The IQ Workout Series

PSYCHOMETRIC TESTING

1000 ways to assess your personality, creativity, intelligence and lateral thinking

Philip Carter and Ken Russell

JOHN WILEY & SONS, LTD

Chichester · New York · Weinheim · Brisbane · Singapore · Toronto

Published 2001 by John Wiley & Sons Ltd,
Baffins Lane, Chichester,
West Sussex PO19 1UD, England

National   01243 779777
International (+44) 1243 779777
e-mail (for orders and customer service enquiries):
cs-books@wiley.co.uk
Visit our Home Page on http://www.wiley.co.uk
or http://www.wiley.com

Other Wiley Editorial Offices

John Wiley & Sons, Inc., 605 Third Avenue,
New York, NY 10158-0012, USA

WILEY-VCH Verlag GmbH, Pappelallee 3,
D-69469 Weinheim, Germany

John Wiley & Sons Australia Ltd, 33 Park Road, Milton,
Queensland 4064, Australia

John Wiley & Sons (Asia) Pte Ltd, 2 Clementi Loop #02-01,
Jin Xing Distripark, Singapore 129809

John Wiley & Sons (Canada) Ltd, 22 Worcester Road,
Rexdale, Ontario M9W 1L1, Canada

British Library Cataloguing in Publication Data

A catalogue record for this book is available from the British Library

ISBN 0-471-52376-3

Typeset in 11/14 pt Garamond Book by Dorwyn Ltd, Rowlands Castle, Hants.
Printed and bound in Great Britain by Biddles Ltd, Guildford and King's Lynn.

This book is printed on acid-free paper responsibly manufactured from sustainable forestry, in which at least two trees are planted for each one used for paper production.

Contents

Introduction

Psychometric tests have existed since the beginning of the 20th century. In the past 25–30 years they have been brought into widespread use in industry because of the need of employers to ensure that they place the right people in the right job from the outset. One of the main reasons for this is the high cost of errors, including the need to re-advertise and interview new applicants, and reinvestment in training.

The British Psychological Society defines a psychometric test as: 'an instrument designed to produce a quantitive assessment of some psychological attribute or attributes'.

The use of psychometric testing in selection is now well established, and it can be used to provide objective information about different areas of candidates' skills, for example, the extent of their knowledge, motivations, personality and potential.

The two main types of psychometric tests used are personality questionnaires and aptitude tests.

Personality refers to the patterns of thought, feeling and behaviour that are unique to every one of us, and these are the characteristics that distinguish us from other people. Our personality implies the predictability of how we are likely to act or react under different circumstances.

In reality, of course, nothing is that simple and our reactions to situations are never so predictable. In many ways, the word personality defies a simple definition, so broad is its usage.

Although through the years theorists have emphasised different aspects of personality, and have disagreed about its development and its effect on behaviour, it is accepted generally that heredity and development combine and interact to form our basic personality.

In addition to heredity, many psychologists believe that critical periods exist in personality development, when we are most sensitive to a particular type of environmental event, for example when we are developing our understanding of language. How well our basic needs are met in infancy can also leave a permanent mark on our personality.

Very loosely, a **personality test** is any device or instrument for assessing or evaluating personality.

Although personality questionnaires are usually referred to as tests, this can be misleading as they do not have pass or fail scores. They are designed to measure attitudes, habits and values, and are not usually timed. Sometimes these questionnaires are incorporated into the employer's application form and sometimes they are used during the second-stage procedure.

The personality tests in the first half of this book are designed to measure a range of aspects of your character and make-up in a fun, lighthearted and entertaining way. Although preparation or practice does not affect the outcome of this type of questionnaire, it can nevertheless be a useful exercise to use these tests to analyse yourself from time to time, and also have fun analysing your friends and family.

There is no need to read through these tests first before attempting them: just answer intuitively, and without too much consideration. There are no right or wrong responses.

Whenever you are faced with a personality questionnaire, then it is necessary to answer the questions correctly. Any attempt to guess what you think is the correct answer, in other words the answer that you think your prospective employer wants to see, will often be spotted when your answers are being analysed. At all times, simply follow the instructions and be honest with your answers.

Aptitude tests, or as they are perhaps better known, intelligence tests, are designed to give an objective assessment of the candidate's abilities in a number of disciplines, for example, in verbal understanding, numeracy, logic, and spatial or diagrammatic reasoning skills. Unlike personality tests, aptitude tests are marked and may have a cut-off point above which you pass, and below which you fail or need to be assessed again. Intelligence tests, or IQ (intelligence quotient) tests are standardised after being given to many thousands of people and an average IQ (100) established. A score above or below this norm is used, according to a bell curve, to establish the subject's actual IQ rating.

While it is accepted that IQ is hereditary and remains constant throughout life, and, therefore, it is not possible to increase your actual IQ, it is possible to improve your performance on IQ tests by practising the many different types of question, and learning to recognise the recurring themes. The aptitude tests in the second part of this book are typical of the type and style of question you are likely to encounter in actual tests and will provide valuable practice for anyone who may have to take this type of test in the future.

Employers use aptitude tests to find out if the candidate has the ability to fit the required vacancy, and these tests can also be used to identify suitable jobs for people within an organisation. These tests can be helpful to both the employer and the candidate in identifying strengths and weaknesses, and thus help to find the job for which the person is most suited.

Psychometric testing is likely to become even more popular and widely used by employers in the future. In the USA, the Graduate Record Examination for graduate entry into universities is being replaced over the next few years by a Computer Adaptive Test, which is an interactive form of testing where the questions are set in relation to the ease with which questions have been answered. It is likely that computerised testing will become the norm in the future, and students will have ample opportunity to practise on similar tests in the coming years as sample tests proliferate on the Internet.

Section 1
Personality tests

Personality test one

In each of the following, tick just one word from the three alternatives provided which you think is most applicable to yourself. You must make a choice in each case to obtain an accurate assessment. If you are unsure of the exact meaning of any word it is advisable to look it up in a dictionary, as this will, in fact, make your score a more valid one.

1
a) variable
b) sure
c) adequate

2
a) sophisticated
b) vigorous
c) tolerable

3
a) hesitant
b) tenacious
c) popular

4
a) resisting
b) enduring
c) balanced

5
a) shy
b) solid
c) rational

6
a) tentative
b) firm
c) general

7
a) fluctuating
b) resolute
c) habitual

8
a) open
b) concentrated
c) typical

9
a) suspicious
b) straight
c) unexceptional

10
a) speculative
b) durable
c) decent

11
a) controversial
b) hardy
c) respectable

12
a) unsettled
b) audacious
c) reputable

13
a) restless
b) assured
c) proper

14
a) fidgity
b) definite
c) sufficient

15
a) peaceful
b) emphatic
c) able

16
a) nervous
b) decisive
c) tidy

17
a) cautious
b) tough
c) moderate

18
a) excitable
b) forward
c) conscientious

19
a) unpredictable
b) undaunted
c) impartial

20
a) changeable
b) steadfast
c) conforming

21
a) cryptic
b) spirited
c) capable

22
a) ambivalent
b) vivacious
c) punctual

23
a) content
b) effervescent
c) faithful

24
a) unhappy
b) resilient
c) accurate

25
a) unlikely
b) buoyant
c) just

Assessment

Award yourself 0 points for every 'a' answer, 2 points for every 'b', and 1 point for every 'c'.

40–50 points
An extremely strong personality.

Keywords: tough, ambitious, assertive.

You are likely to know exactly what you want in life and not rest until you achieve your goals.

You are likely to be a success, but are likely to become frustrated if you do not achieve your targets.

25–39 points
A very balanced personality in terms of strength.

Keywords: considerate, tolerant, kind.

In the main, your score indicates that you are as supportive of others as you are ambitious for your own aspirations. You are a good team player, and you know what you want out of life, but are prepared to accept the inevitable downs as well as the ups.

Less than 25
Less than strong personality.

Keywords: indecisive, tentative, irresolute.

Your score does indicate a lack of confidence and doubt in your own abilities. While you may be at peace with the world and content with your lot, this may mean that you are not exploiting your potential sufficiently. It may be to your advantage to set yourself higher goals and realise that you have just as much talent and ability to succeed in life as the next person.

Personality test two

In each of the following, tick just one word from the two alternatives provided which you think is more applicable to yourself. You must make a choice in each case to obtain an accurate assessment. If you are unsure of the exact meaning of any word it is advisable to look it up in a dictionary, as this will, in fact, make your score a more valid one.

1
a) sensitive
b) detached

2
a) softhearted
b) reserved

3
a) sympathetic
b) discreet

4
a) passionate
b) judicious

5
a) responsive
b) prudent

6
a) susceptible
b) dependable

7
a) impressionable
b) staunch

8
a) instinctive
b) reflective

9
a) receptive
b) calculating

10
a) perceptive
b) leisurely

11
a) vulnerable
b) deliberate

12
a) touchy
b) formal

13
a) volatile
b) casual

14
a) erratic
b) restrained

15
a) whimsical
b) diffident

16
a) careless
b) conventional

17
a) outgoing
b) reticent

18
a) zany
b) withdrawn

19
a) changeable
b) secretive

20
a) impetuous
b) modest

21
a) hurried
b) unaffected

22
a) impulsive
b) practical

23
a) poignant
b) logical

24
a) expressive
b) analytical

25
a) demonstrative
b) subtle

Assessment

Award yourself 0 points for every 'a' answer and 2 points for every 'b' answer.

40–50 points
Exceptionally unemotional.

Keywords: stable, confident, secure.

You are unusually stable and likely to keep your head in a crisis, while all around you are losing theirs.

This is fine so long as you do not bottle up your emotions to the extent that you worry inwardly all the time, as this can be harmful to your health and well-being.

24–39 points
You have an average degree of emotionality.

Keywords: well-adjusted, temperate.

You are not immune to worrying and occasionally show the odd display of emotion, but this is the exception rather than the rule.

Less than 24
Your score indicates that you are highly emotional.

Keywords: hurried, passionate, sentimental, excitable, anxious.

You are likely to feel somewhat stressed out by life. This makes you vulnerable both to life's negative and positive aspects, and often you are thus deeply affected by tragedy and joy alike and make no attempt to contain your reactions to these events within yourself.

In expressing these emotions you are respected by your family and colleagues as a person of great sensitivity, and this quality of vulnerability endears many people to you.

The term 'emotion' is one which is most familiarly used as being synonymous with feeling. The three main reactions of emotion are anger, love and fear, which occur as a result of either some external event, or an indirect process such as memory or association. Such reaction can manifest itself within the individual by means of an accelerated or reduced pulse rate, increased activity of certain glands or a change in body temperature.

The reaction generally diminishes in proportion to the maturity of the individual. These causes of different types of emotional reaction also become more complex with maturity; for example, what causes anger in a child may cause a different type of emotion, fear, in an adult.

Our reactions too will differ in each one of us. For example, fear may manifest itself physically in some people by the quaking of limbs, shakiness or even loss of speech. In others the same emotion may disguise itself by means of assumed coolness or bravado.

Personality test three

In each of the following, tick just one word from the two alternatives provided which you think is more applicable to yourself. You must make a choice in each case to obtain an accurate assessment. If you are unsure of the exact meaning of any word it is advisable to look it up in a dictionary, as this will, in fact, make your score a more valid one.

1
a) satisfied
b) angry

2
a) pleased
b) restless

3
a) moderate
b) variable

4
a) soft
b) temperamental

5
a) happy
b) insecure

6
a) lucky
b) hesitant

7
a) fit
b) cautious

8
a) adjusted
b) fidgety

9
a) adequate
b) uneasy

10
a) blithe
b) pliant

11
a) lighthearted
b) changeable

12
a) lively
b) nervous

13
a) vigorous
b) impetuous

14
a) dynamic
b) uncertain

15
a) robust
b) frivolous

16
a) reconciled
b) roving

17
a) cheerful
b) anxious

18
a) steady
b) rash

19
a) loving
b) confused

20
a) tough
b) tense

21
a) balanced
b) concerned

22
a) devoted
b) stubborn

23
a) cordial
b) uptight

24
a) considerate
b) rigid

25
a) demonstrative
b) headstrong

Assessment

Award yourself 2 points for every 'a' answer and 0 points for every 'b' answer.

40–50 points

You are very content with your life, and as such are likely to be a very happy person, and this happiness rubs off on those around you, especially your immediate family.

Perhaps it does mean that you lack ambition because you are satisfied with your lot in life, but if you are so satisfied and content, why is there the need to try for anything more out of life? Increased success does not necessarily bring with it increased happiness; in fact, the reverse can often be the case.

Keywords: contentment, happiness, inner peace, relaxed.

24–39 points

You are content with your life, although sometimes you may not realise it just as much as you ought to.

While you do not lack ambition, you would never wish to realise such ambitions at the expense of your happiness and your settled lifestyle, and the happiness of your family. There is, however, always a feeling at the back of your mind that you could do more, and at times you find this a little frustrating.

Keywords: satisfied, thoughtful, fulfilled.

Less than 24

You are in the main discontent with your life. Perhaps you feel that you have not fulfilled your ambitions or yet realised your full potential. Perhaps you think that life is all too short and that you have not enough time to do all the things you always wanted to do.

Perhaps now might be a good time to step back and take stock of your life. What have you achieved? Perhaps you have a steady job and a loving and stable family life. These are in themselves no mean achievements in life. Perhaps you have a hobby that you are good at, again no mean achievement.

All in all, there are so many things in all our lives that we can be thankful for. If you are able to focus more on all the positive things in your life, no matter how trivial or insignificant they may seem, then there is every chance that you will find the inner peace and satisfaction that has so eluded you in the past.

Keywords: frustrated, despondent, exasperated, disappointed.

How confident are you?

1 How much confidence have you in your own decisions?

  a) a great deal
  b) usually fairly confident
  c) not always confident as I tend to worry whether I
     have made the correct decision

2 If you were asked to be best man at your friend's
  wedding, how much would you worry about the speech
  you would have to make?

  a) not at all
  b) perhaps a little
  c) quite a lot

3 How often have you proposed a vote of thanks at a
  meeting?

  a) several times
  b) once
  c) never

4 Do you prefer to circulate and talk to strangers at social
  gatherings, or stay within your own circle of
  acquaintances?

a) circulate
b) no preference, I do both
c) stay within my own circle of friends

5 Would you be very nervous at the prospect of meeting royalty?

a) no
b) a little nervous
c) very nervous

6 How often do you worry about your appearance?

a) never
b) occasionally
c) often

7 Do you think people see you as a very positive person?

a) yes
b) I hope so
c) no

8 Do you usually play sport to win, or purely for the enjoyment?

a) I always play to win
b) for both
c) purely for the enjoyment

9 Have you ever applied to take part in a television quiz show?

a) yes
b) I have thought about it but never got round to it
c) no, never even thought about it

10 How would you feel about giving a talk about something on which you are very knowledgeable to your local Women's Institute?

    a) no problem
    b) it is not something I would relish, but if asked I might accept
    c) I would not want to do it at all

11 Do you like to talk to influential people whenever you can?

    a) yes
    b) I wouldn't go out of my way to talk to them
    c) no

12 Do you believe in the power of positive thinking?

    a) yes
    b) sometimes
    c) no, fate will deal you whatever hand it wants, whatever your aspirations

13 Have you ever phoned a television or radio station to take part in a topical debate?

    a) yes
    b) no, but I wouldn't rule out the possibility of doing so in the future
    c) no, and I don't expect I ever will

14 How often have you told your boss that you do not agree with the way he or she is doing things?

    a) several times
    b) only very occasionally
    c) never

15 You are taking part in an argument with several people and it appears they all hold strongly opposing views to yourself. If you are totally convinced you are correct which of the following is likely to be your reaction to this situation?

   a) relish the debate and try even harder to put your point of view across
   b) stick to your guns but end the argument quickly by making a comment such as 'we will have to agree to differ on this'
   c) give up the argument and start to think that you might not be correct after all

16 Would you do a bungee jump for charity?

   a) yes
   b) I might, but would be terrified at the prospect
   c) no

17 You have been queueing for an hour for some train tickets and when you reach the counter the clerk is particularly unhelpful and negative. Which of the following is most likely to be your reaction?

   a) ask to see the person in charge and complain bitterly, even though this may take place in front of a large number of people still queueing behind you
   b) just complain to the clerk that you think he or she is being unhelpful
   c) don't complain, but persevere quietly until the clerk fully understands what you want, even if this takes another half hour

18 How often have you backed the underdog in an argument?

a) often, and I always will if I think they are correct
b) occasionally
c) very rarely, I usually keep out of strong arguments

19 Do you enjoy flirting with members of the opposite sex?

a) yes, quite a lot
b) yes, occasionally
c) not really

20 How nervous are you about other people seeing you naked?

a) not at all
b) a little
c) very nervous

21 Have you a party piece that you like to perform at family Christmas gatherings?

a) yes
b) not a party piece as such, but if forced into it I will take my turn and sing something solo or tell a joke
c) no

22 Do you like to drive at very high speed on an open road?

a) yes, as fast as I can get away with
b) occasionally I have exceeded the speed limit on the motorway
c) no, driving at very high speed scares me somewhat

23 When you buy a lottery ticket, how high are your expectations about winning?

a) I know the odds but have quite high expectations that one day I will have a very big win
b) I am quite hopeful that I will win one of the lesser prizes
c) not at all hopeful, but if I do win it will be a wonderful surprise

24 How nervous are you about taking a plane journey?

a) not at all nervous as, statistically, it is one of the safest forms of transport
b) quite nervous
c) more than nervous, terrified would be a better description

25 You are told that there is to be a complete reorganisation in the company where you work. What are your feelings about this?

a) I would like to be involved in the reorganisation if possible as it may provide me with a better career opportunity
b) somewhat apprehensive as I am happy with things as they are
c) quite alarmed as it may mean redundancies or changes to my job description

Assessment

Award yourself 2 points for every 'a' answer, 1 point for every 'b' and 0 points for every 'c'.

35–50 points
You are brimming over with confidence and have total belief in your own ability in almost everything you do.

The only thing you need to be wary of is over-confidence as success is something which needs to be worked hard for and does not happen just because you expect it to.

Also, because you are not backward in coming forward, you may be seen as brash or cocky by many people, who think you may be riding for a fall and are eagerly awaiting the day when this happens.

Keywords: presumptuous, extrovert, sure.

16–34 points

Your score indicates that you are generally a confident person with a positive outlook on life.

Because you are not the over-confident type, this is likely to make you popular with all your friends and colleagues, with whom you are able to interact on an equal basis, without giving anyone an inferiority complex.

Keywords: secure, positive, sensible.

Below 16

You appear to lack a great deal of confidence in your own abilities and are likely to be over-modest about your achievements.

Modesty is admired by many people, especially if they know that you have demonstrated more ability, and achieved much more, than you give yourself credit for. Nevertheless, it may be a good idea to sit back and evaluate just what you have achieved in life, and what talents you possess, compared with those people who appear so self-assured. You may well surprise yourself by such an analysis, and it may make you believe much more in your own abilities in the future.

Keywords: diffident, pessimistic, modest, introverted.

Are you tactful or undiplomatic?

1 You are at a party and a crushing bore corners you. In which of the following ways are you most likely to extricate yourself from this situation?

   a) start yawning or looking bored, then if the person doesn't get the message make an excuse to do something else such as make a telephone call
   b) make an excuse that you have just seen someone at the other side of the room you have to talk to about something
   c) politely listen, but try to change the subject to something that your companion might find equally boring, in the hopes that he or she will move away to bore someone else

2 A work colleague comes into the office one morning wearing a particularly garish and inappropriate item of clothing. Which of the following is most likely to be your reaction?

   a) a comment such as 'I expect you must be wearing that to win a bet'
   b) a comment such as 'well, that's different'
   c) say nothing and keep your thoughts to yourself

3 You see in the evening paper that a colleague has been banned from driving for 12 months for drunk driving.

Which of the following is most likely to be the way you handle this knowledge the next time you see your colleague?

a) come straight out with the fact that you have seen it in the paper so as to clear the air immediately

b) make a jokey comment such as 'I don't suppose you could give me a lift home tonight in your car, could you?'

c) say nothing, and leave it to your colleague to raise the subject

4 Some friends invite you over for dinner and the main meal is something you detest eating. Which of the following is most likely to be your reaction?

a) apologise profusely and say that you simply cannot eat this type of food but you do appreciate all the trouble they have gone to

b) make a valiant attempt to eat what you can

c) eat what you can and complement your host on the quality of anything on the plate which you were able to eat

5 A relative buys you a particularly horrendous vase. Which of the following is most likely to be your reaction?

a) 'Good grief! What have I done to deserve that?'

b) 'Thank you very much, but actually it is not quite to my taste. Is there any chance of taking it back to the shop and exchanging it?'

c) 'It is really very nice. I will have to try and find a place for it.'

6 You meet an old friend whom you haven't seen for some time, who looks terribly ill. Which of the following is most likely to be your reaction?

a) 'Oh my God, you look terrible. What's the problem?'
b) make a comment to the effect, 'how have you been keeping recently?'
c) make a fuss and say how delighted you are to see them, but make no mention of their obvious ill health unless they care to broach the subject first

7 Your neighbour has some conifers that are blocking all the light to your house. In which of the following ways would you initially convey that you would prefer the offending trees to be trimmed?

a) drop a few hints when you are in the garden so that your neighbour can overhear, such as 'it's dark round here isn't it?' or 'it's like the movie *Day of the Triffids* round here'
b) when your neighbour is out, put a leaflet through the door from a local company that specialises in trimming conifers
c) be honest, and say that while you admire the conifers greatly, is there any chance of your neighbour trimming them back because they are blocking the light to your house

8 You are walking along the street and someone approaching you falls full length. How would you react?

a) make a humorous comment to try and lighten their possible embarrassment, such as 'see you next fall' or 'enjoy your next trip'
b) do nothing unless they appear to have hurt themselves
c) rush to their aid and ask if they are OK and whether there is anything you can do to help

9 You visit some friends and their garden is a terrible mess. What is most likely to be your reaction?

   a) make a comment such as 'it's a jungle out there, isn't it?', or 'I see gardening is not one of your strong points'
   b) make a comment such as 'I expect you have been too busy with your work recently to get round to all your jobs'
   c) make no comment whatsoever about the state of the garden

10 You go out for an expensive meal twice a year with some ex-neighbours and pay alternately. You are due to go for your next meal in two weeks time and it is your ex-neighbours' turn to pay. Then you learn that one of them has suddenly lost their job and is out of work. How would you handle this situation?

   a) phone them up and ask them if they wish to cancel the meal
   b) phone them up and say that you would still like to go for the meal, but under the circumstances you hope they will let you pay even though it is not your turn
   c) do nothing and let the arrangement stand

11 Your friend's first book has just been published, and it has been panned by the critics. What is most likely to be your reaction the next time you see your friend?

   a) 'I see the book didn't go down too well then?'
   b) 'Don't worry about what the critics say, I'm sure it will sell very well'
   c) 'Congratulations on the publication of your book. Any chance of a signed copy?'

12 A work colleague has just suffered a bereavement. How would you handle this situation the next time you meet up, which is several days after the funeral?

   a) make a comment such as 'how are you now? I hope the funeral went OK'
   b) say nothing
   c) take your colleague to one side at a quiet and private moment, offer your sympathies and say how sorry you were to hear about the bad news

13 A neighbour has just been made redundant. What do you say the next time you meet up?

   a) 'I expect you are pretty cut up about losing your job. It's a sad reflection of our times when things like this happen'
   b) 'Look on the bright side, things like this often work out for the best'
   c) say nothing about the redundancy

14 You are washing your car in the drive and your neighbour arrives back home with a severely dented new car. Which is most likely to be your reaction?

   a) a semi-humorous comment to break the ice such as 'I hope you are well insured'
   b) a comment such as 'oops! what's the other chap's car like?'
   c) a comment such as 'oh dear, sorry to see you have had an accident, are you OK?'

15 You are at the works Christmas party and someone of the opposite sex whom you particularly dislike starts to chat you up. Assuming you are single and carefree, which of the following is most likely to be your reaction?

a) tell them in no uncertain terms to go and bother someone else as they are wasting their time trying it on with you

b) tell them straight that they are just not your type, so as to avoid them wasting any more of both your time and theirs

c) try to chat to them a little to get to know them more, as there is a chance you may have misjudged them in the past.

16 A colleague comes to work in odd shoes, one black and one brown, and you are the first to notice. What is most likely to be your reaction?

a) tell your other colleagues first that you have just seen something very funny

b) make a comment like, 'have you another pair of shoes like that at home?'

c) take them to one side and tell them about it so as to give them a chance to go home and change before someone else notices

17 A work colleague announces that he has decided to undergo a sex change. The next day he arrives at work in women's clothes as the first stage of his changeover. What is most likely to be your reaction the first time you see him?

a) 'Oh no! I didn't think you were serious. Are you sure you have thought through what you are doing?'

b) 'Wow, I admire your courage, good luck to you. I hope people will treat you the same as they always have done in the past'

c) say nothing different to what you would say any other day

18 A new member of staff is becoming increasingly loud and
obnoxious. Which of the following do you think is the
most effective way to deal with this, in the first instance,
if you are the departmental manager?

a) tell him he is not fitting in and that you may have to
consider his future if he persists with this type of
behaviour

b) tell him that while his work is satisfactory you have
noticed that he has on occasions upset other
members of staff, and advise him to think about this
carefully

c) tell him that you have noticed that his behaviour has
been upsetting other members of staff, and ask him if
he would like any help with sorting this out, or if he
has any personal problems he would like to talk to
you about

19 A colleague arrives at work one day sporting a black eye.
How would you react to this?

a) make a comment like, 'what's the other chap like?'

b) ask them if they have had some sort of accident

c) say nothing

20 Do you consider that yours is a good shoulder to cry on?

a) not particularly

b) I hope so

c) yes

21 Your friend brings a banjo round to your Christmas party
and starts doing George Formby impressions which,
quite frankly, are terrible. How would you handle this
situation?

a) suggest a vote of the guests on whether the impressions should continue by popular demand, or whether the banjo should be consigned to the dustbin for all time
b) start to heckle and boo jokingly, and hope that your friend will get the message
c) say that you are putting some disco music on by popular demand

22 You are in a restaurant at quite a small table and someone sitting opposite is obviously struggling to fit their plate on the table. You offer to help by clearing the table to make more room but they make a somewhat snobbish comment that they can manage perfectly well themselves and they are not likely to finish up eating out of their lap. Sure enough, a minute later, the plate, together with the food, well garnished with tomato ketchup, upturns onto their lap. What is most likely to be your reaction?

a) you would simply not be able to keep your face straight and would not even attempt to do so
b) you would try to keep your face straight but would probably fail in the attempt and go red in the face in your efforts
c) you would gallantly dash round to their rescue with a pile of napkins to help them mop up the mess

23 You are in the garden one summer and your neighbour's dog comes into the garden and starts fouling the middle of your beautifully manicured lawn. How are you most likely to react?

a) tell your neighbour what has happened in no uncertain terms

b) yell at the dog 'get out of it!' even though your neighbour may be within earshot

c) clean up the mess and hope it doesn't happen again

24 You are walking along the street and someone who obviously knows you stops to have a chat. Unfortunately you cannot place the person. How are you most likely to handle this situation?

a) say, 'do I know you?'

b) after a while say something to the effect, 'I'm sorry this is really embarrassing but although I do know you I have just forgotten your name'

c) don't tell them that you cannot place them

25 You walk into the office and are told that someone has just fallen backwards off their chair. Which of the following is most likely to be your immediate reaction toward them?

a) 'I missed that, can you do it again?'

b) 'Are you OK?'

c) make no comment directly to them about it

Assessment

Award yourself 0 points for every 'a' answer, 1 point for every 'b' and 2 points for every 'c'.

35–50 points

You are extremely tactful and the soul of discretion, always making sure you go to great lengths not to hurt other people's feelings.

This does mean that on occasions you are not perfectly honest with people, but to you that is more important than hurting their feelings, and then having to live with your own feelings of guilt that you might have upset them.

16–34 points

You can be tactful, but at other times are unable to stop yourself from saying things that you might regret later, or that you think people to whom you are directing your remarks would be better off hearing.

You are, however, in the fortunate position of usually knowing just when, and when not, things are better said or better left, and usually your good judgement in these matters will prove beneficial to the person to whom you are directing your remarks, and you would never deliberately go out of your way to upset someone.

Below 16

Unfortunately, your score indicates that tact is not one of your strong points and you do not suffer fools gladly. You are most unlikely to make a successful career as a diplomat or in public relations.

While you do not lack honesty, you do appear to have little concern for other people's feelings, whether you do this intentionally or as a means of actually mischievously trying to wind people up on occasions, and having a laugh at their expense.

It may be beneficial to think about and reflect on your answers to some of the above questions very carefully and what your feelings would be if the roles were reversed. Would your feeling have suffered had you been on the receiving end of some of these reactions and responses, and if so, is it worth on future occasions being much more discreet?

Laterality

If we were to remove a human brain from the skull we would see that it is made up of two almost identical hemispheres. Each of these halves seems to have developed specialised functions and has its own private sensations, perceptions, thoughts and ideas.

The term *laterality* is used to refer to any one of a number of preferences for one side of the body over another.

The following test is designed to discover whether you are basically a right-sided brain person or a left-sided brain person and to identify the strengths and weaknesses of one-hemisphere dominance.

1 Do you find it easier to remember people's names or faces?

   a) names
   b) both equally
   c) faces

2 Which of these describes your attitude to failure?
   a) try, try and try again
   b) it can be soul destroying
   c) give up and try something new

3 How often do you follow your hunches?

   a) rarely
   b) sometimes
   c) whenever I can

4 If you suddenly had an urge to try a new creative hobby such as painting or pottery, what would you be most likely to do about it?

   a) probably go no further than thinking about it
   b) probably try it a few times then move onto something else
   c) try it and perhaps develop it as one of my many hobbies

5 Would you call yourself an organised person?

   a) very much so
   b) reasonably so
   c) not at all

6 With which of the following subjects did you feel most comfortable at school?

   a) mathematics
   b) geography
   c) art

7 With which of the following statements can you most identify?

   a) I am happy to abide by rules and regulations
   b) rules and regulations sometimes annoy me
   c) I like to make my own rules

8 How often do you like to move the furniture around in your home?

   a) less than once every five years
   b) two or three times every five years
   c) more than three times every five years

9 Which of the following most grabs your attention when watching the news on television?

   a) politics
   b) sport
   c) global and environmental issues

10 When you are attending a talk or lecture which of the following do you find?

   a) I am able to focus my concentration on the speaker
   b) I am only able to maintain my concentration if I find the subject interesting
   c) I often find myself drifting off and thinking about other things

11 Which of these words do you feel best describes you?

   a) studious
   b) thorough
   c) intuitive

12 Which of these do you feel best sums you up?

   a) someone who is ambitious
   b) someone who has good common sense
   c) someone who has a lively imagination

13 Would you call yourself a specialist?

 a) yes
 b) in some respects
 c) no

14 What is your opinion of modern art?

 a) I don't care for it very much
 b) I can take it or leave it
 c) I find it interesting

15 What do you see as the main advantage to being retired?

 a) having more time to spend with family and friends
 b) freedom from disciplined routine
 c) having the time to pursue many new activities

16 Which of the following is most applicable to yourself?

 a) down-to-earth
 b) typical
 c) complex

17 How often do you retire into your own private thoughts
 for a 'thinking session'?

 a) very rarely
 b) occasionally
 c) more than occasionally

18 When you walk into an auditorium without a reserved
 ticket and there are seats available either side, which side
 do you normally prefer?

a) the right side
b) no preference
c) the left side

19 Which of these words is most applicable to yourself ?

a) stressed
b) busy
c) thoughtful

20 Are you generally able to tell approximately how much time has passed without looking at your watch?

a) yes, usually I do have a fairly good idea
b) sometimes
c) to be honest I wouldn't really have much idea how much time had passed as I usually lose track of time completely

21 Which of the following most frustrates you?

a) not being at the top of my profession
b) not being given recognition for my achievements and hard work
c) not having the time to do all the things I would like to do

22 What do you think about the statement 'the greatest teacher is experience'?

a) don't agree
b) agree
c) strongly agree

23 Ideally, which of the following types of working day
would you prefer?:

a) a set routine
b) one that provides you with the opportunity to learn
something new
c) one that is completely unpredictable with many new
experiences

24 Do you consider yourself a good speller?

a) yes
b) average
c) no

25 With which of the following tasks would you feel most
comfortable?

a) writing a letter or report
b) performing a manual task such as painting and
decorating
c) performing a more skilled task such as tinkering with
your car's engine

Assessment

Award yourself 0 points for every 'a' answer, 1 point for
every 'b' and 2 points for every 'c'.

35–50 points
This score indicates that you are very much a right-sided
brain person. It is the right side of our brain which controls
spatial ability, artistic appreciation and creative thought.
    The right side is the intuitive hemisphere, which imagines
and perceives things holistically. In other words, you like to

see the big picture, rather than seeing the component details. As such, it is the side of the brain that reconstructs a whole pattern out of individual pieces, at the same time giving rise to new ideas and concepts.

It is also likely that as a right-brained person you have an appreciation of art and music and have an interest in the exploration of ritual and mysticism. As a predominantly right-sided brain person you tend to learn in a subconscious and creative way, leading to an emotional reaction to situations as opposed to a detailed and logical analysis. On many occasions it is likely that you have arrived at the correct answer to a question or problem without being sure how the answer was arrived at: this is where intuition is so important to the right-sided brain person.

The left brain tends to process things in sequence as opposed to the right-brain approach, which is random. Therefore, as a right-sided brain person you may find that you have a tendency to move from one task to another before the first task is completed. As this can sometimes be a disadvantage, because you can find yourself with several tasks all uncompleted, it may assist to start making lists and schedules in order to discipline yourself to complete tasks more efficiently without flitting from one assignment to another

16–34 points

Your score indicates that you have the right balance between the right and left brain hemispheres without being particularly dominated by either side.

While this can be a considerable advantage it is, nevertheless, no cause for complacency.

One problem with hemispherical balance is that you will possibly tend to feel more conflict than someone with clearly established dominance. Occasionally this conflict will be between what you feel and what you think, and it will also involve how you tackle problems and interpret information. Sometimes details which seem important to the right hemisphere will be discounted by the left and vice versa, and this can be a hindrance to an efficient learning process or the completion of tasks.

On the positive side, the advantage of having a balanced brain is that with problem solving you can perceive the big picture and the essential details simultaneously. You are also likely to possess sufficient verbal skills to translate your intuition into a form that can be understood by others while still being able to access ideas of a more spatial nature.

It is of great advantage to balanced brain individuals that they have the natural ability to succeed in multiple fields due to the great flexibility of mind which they possess.

Below 16

Your score indicates that you are a predominantly left-sided brain dominated person.

For most people the left side of the brain is analytical and functions in a sequential and rational fashion and is the side which controls language, academic studies and rationality.

The left-brain person will tend to process information in a linear manner, in other words from part to whole, as opposed to the right-sided brain person, who likes to visualise the big picture first.

The left brain also tends to process things in sequence as opposed to the random processing of the right brain. Accordingly the left-brain person is likely to be a fine master scheduler or accountant. Also spelling is likely to be a strong point of the left-brain person, as spelling involves sequencing.

It may be to the advantage of the predominantly left-brain person to employ certain right-brain strategies, in particular the development of creative thinking skills and intuition. In the classroom, for example, a right-brain student may be at a disadvantage when attending a lecture unless they have been given an overview of the whole concept first as they essentially need to know exactly what they are doing and why. On the other hand, the left-brain student may not find it necessary to look this far ahead, but perhaps would find it helpful to do so.

The right and left hemisphere functions can be summarised as follows:

Left hemisphere	Right hemisphere
parsing	holistic
logic	intuition
conscious thought	subconscious thought
outer awareness	inner awareness
methods, rules	creativity
written language	insight
number skills	three-dimensional forms
reasoning	imagination
scientific skills	music, art
aggression	passive
sequential	simultaneous
verbal intelligence	practical intelligence
intellectual	sensuousness
analytical	synthetic

Are you likely to be a success?

1 Do you find it easy to concentrate on one subject?

   a) not at all, I like to diversify my interests
   b) I try hard but it's difficult at times
   c) yes, I have no problem doing this

2 Do you ever find that your hobby interferes with your day job?

   a) yes, often
   b) sometimes
   c) never

3 You are looking forward to a weekend at home with the family when suddenly an urgent job crops up on a Friday afternoon. What is your reaction?

   a) you say it will have to wait as you have already made plans for the weekend
   b) you try to get someone else to do the job for you
   c) you forfeit your weekend to get the job done

4 You move to a new job and the local polytechnic is advertising a course which is very relevant to the job you are doing. How would you react?

a) not really be interested in going on the course
b) only go on the course if it was paid for by the company
c) be very interested in going on the course even if you had to pay for it yourself

5 You are feeling particularly unwell one morning and wonder if you are coming down with a heavy cold or even the flu. How would you behave?

a) certify yourself sick and hope that you can shake it off by having a day at home
b) go to the surgery and ask for the doctor's opinion on whether you are fit for work
c) go to work and struggle on for as long as you can

6 How often do you grumble about the company you work for to friends and family?

a) often
b) sometimes
c) very rarely

7 Where do you see yourself in five years' time?

a) probably doing the same job
b) hopefully in some sort of better position
c) I fully intend having advanced my career considerably in the next five years

8 You are asked to go on a residential training course which happens to be just five miles from your home address. What do you say?

a) I will go on the course but as it is so near where I live I will not stay overnight
b) I will go on the course but will only stay overnight if the company prefer me to
c) I will stay overnight because I am part of a team and don't want to be the odd one out

9 Do you feel grumpy early in the morning?

a) only when it's a working day
b) I do sometimes
c) Very rarely. I regard every day as an exciting new challenge

10 Do you talk about your job outside work?

a) no, I turn off as quickly as I can at the end of each working day
b) I do sometimes
c) very frequently

11 Are you doing the job you always knew you wanted to do?

a) not at all
b) I perhaps thought I might do something along these lines
c) yes, it's what I always planned to do

12 Do you think intelligence leads to success?

a) yes, you must be intelligent to make a success in life
b) it is a big contributory factor
c) intelligence alone doesn't lead to success

13 Do you think you should have six-monthly assessment meetings with your boss?

    a) certainly not, what a waste of time
    b) yes, although I would be very apprehensive before such a meeting
    c) yes, they are an excellent idea and a great opportunity to discuss aspects of my job and career in detail

14 Do you consider yourself ruthless?

    a) no, I don't like people who are ruthless
    b) maybe a little
    c) I'm afraid I am when it comes to getting what I want

15 How to you feel about going for interviews?

    a) terrified
    b) perhaps somewhat nervous
    c) I enjoy interviews, and the opportunity to show people what I'm made of

16 One of your working colleagues gets promoted. How do you feel?

    a) pleased for your colleague
    b) a little envious
    c) quite upset and wanting to find out why it wasn't me and what went wrong

17 What do you think about hard work?

    a) it is very tiring
    b) it's OK as long as you get paid for it
    c) it is a means to an end

18 If you won the lottery jackpot what would you do?

a) retire and live a life of luxury
b) invest in a business and pay someone to run it
c) carry on working on some sort of enterprise

19 Do you like sitting on committees?

a) not really
b) if pressed I have sat on the occasional committee
c) I prefer to be on the committee of any organisation of which I am a member

20 To what use would you prefer to put a particular talent?

a) it would make a nice hobby
b) it's something there to use when the need arises
c) I would try to build a career around it if possible

21 Do you believe that practice makes perfect?

a) no one is perfect
b) people don't have much time to practise at things in this day and age
c) yes, the harder you work at something the better you become

22 Do you believe in the power of hindsight?

a) no, you cannot alter what has gone
b) sometimes, I suppose, but anyone can be wise with hindsight
c) it's important to look back and analyse our mistakes to ensure we don't repeat them in the future

23 Is it important to impress the right people?

   a) no, that's crawling
   b) sometimes
   c) yes

24 Which of these historical characters would you most like
    to shake the hand of and congratulate?

   a) Casanova
   b) Jesse James
   c) Robert the Bruce

25 From where do you get your motivation?

   a) from my boss
   b) from my immediate family
   c) from within

Assessment

Award yourself 2 points for every 'c' answer, 1 point for
every 'b' and 0 points for every 'a'.

40–50 points

If you aren't a success already then there shouldn't be any
doubts that you will be one day, and if you are already a
success it is likely that you will eventually reach even greater
heights. You have all the qualities necessary for success such
as character, persistence, flair and imagination, and not least
the ambition to push yourself to the heights you know you
are capable of achieving. As long as you take care not to
become a total workaholic at the expense of yourself and
your family, and ultimately your happiness, and can succeed
in striking the right balance, you will successfully reach most

of the goals you have set out to achieve in both your personal and working life.

20–39 points

You do aspire to success and have many of the necessary qualities to achieve this, but perhaps you need to work a little harder at instilling some self-confidence into yourself to make you believe you can, and will, succeed. Perhaps success is something that you dream about but never really believe will happen. It is up to you to translate those dreams into reality and work at removing those self-doubts. You are a hard worker, but is this hard work all in the service of others and not for yourself? If so then try to develop the belief that hard work brings its rewards and that it is about time these rewards were heading in your direction. Having convinced yourself that this is possible then you must set about convincing others. While this is not always easy it is certainly possible, as many have proved.

Less than 20

A great deal of hard work and commitment is required if you are going to make a success in a chosen career. But is this really what you want out of life? You may believe that happiness is more important in life than success and that while happiness for many people is being a high-flyer, for you it may be a stable family life, a steady job with not too much responsibility and a regular monthly salary. Just remember that everyone is their own person and happiness is often not the result of trying to become what you really do not want to be.

Are you a risk taker?

1 What are your views on the old adage, 'You must speculate to accumulate'?

   a) don't agree
   b) it is sometimes true
   c) agree

2 How often do you drive through a red light?

   a) never
   b) occasionally
   c) more than occasionally

3 Have you ever taken part in a dangerous sport?

   a) no
   b) no, but I wouldn't rule out the possibility
   c) yes

4 Are you afraid of flying?

   a) yes
   b) a little
   c) not at all

5 Would you ever make a parachute jump?

  a) no way
  b) maybe
  c) yes

6 You are taking part in the quiz show *Who Wants to be a Millionaire?*. You have just won £64,000. The next question is worth £125,000 if you answer correctly, but if you are wrong you drop back to £32,000. You have narrowed the answer down to two possibilities and are 75% sure of the answer. Would you gamble or walk away with £64,000?

  a) take the money
  b) don't know, it would depend on how I felt at the time
  c) gamble

7 You have been in a steady job for 15 years which provides a decent lifestyle and security for you and your family. One day you are headhunted by a company which offers you 25% more salary but less security. Would you take the new job?

  a) very doubtful
  b) I would consider it very carefully
  c) I probably would

8 How often have you exceeded the 70 miles per hour speed limit on the motorway?

  a) never
  b) occasionally
  c) more than occasionally

9 Do you believe in taking calculated risks?

a) no
b) occasionally
c) yes

10 Which of the following most accurately represents your views on insurance?

a) I believe in over-insurance rather than under-insurance
b) I insure where necessary and where it is prudent to do so
c) insurance is a necessary evil

11 Have you ever done something daring and risky that you hoped no one would find out about?

a) not that I can recall
b) I suppose I have occasionally
c) yes, in fact it gave me something of a kick

12 Would you ever climb on your house roof to repair tiles?

a) no way
b) I might, but would be quite apprehensive
c) it would not worry me in the slightest

13 You have booked a holiday in London and two days before you are due to go, two terrorist bombs are exploded. Would you still take the holiday?

a) no, I would probably cancel
b) London is a big place and the chances of being

injured are very slight even if another bomb
exploded, therefore I would probably still go

c) I would not dream of cancelling

14 If you were out of work long term and got the offer of a
job that involved danger, such as in the police force or
fire service, would you take the job?

a) no
b) possibly
c) yes

15 When you are a pedestrian do you ever cross a road
when the lights are at red if you can see that the road is
clear?

a) no
b) sometimes
c) always

16 You have won £50,000 on the Premium Bonds and wish
to invest £25,000 of it. Which of the following would you
be most likely to choose

a) plough it back into Premium Bonds
b) highest interest bank or building society account
c) very high interest investment account with a small
   degree of risk

17 A night out at which one of the following most appeals
to you?

a) bingo hall
b) greyhound racing
c) casino

18 Would you ever stake a week's wage on one turn of a card?

a) no way
b) I would have to have had plenty of Dutch courage first
c) yes, how exciting

19 Would you ever leave a very steady, secure but mundane job to do something much less secure but that you really enjoyed?

a) no
b) maybe
c) yes

20 In which of these US cities would you prefer to live?

a) Boston
b) Dallas
c) New York

21 When you first book into a hotel room, do you read the fire regulations?

a) yes
b) sometimes, if I notice them
c) no

22 Would you ever break the law if you had the opportunity, it was considerably to your advantage to do so, and it was almost certain you would get away with it?

a) no, I wouldn't dare even if I wanted to
b) I doubt it, but no one can be absolutely certain unless faced with the circumstances
c) I suspect I would

23 How often have you been on a really terrifying ride at a fun-fair?

a) never or only once
b) more than once but only because I was with friends or family who wanted to take the ride
c) more than once because I really enjoy the thrill and the excitement

24 Would you ever take liberties with your health, such as smoke cigarettes?

a) no
b) I have done in the past, but have learnt it isn't a wise thing to do
c) yes, if you call smoking taking liberties with your health

25 To be described as which of the following would secretly please you most?

a) steady and faithful
b) wise and dependable
c) wild and outrageous

Assessment

Award yourself 2 points for every 'c' answer, 1 point for every 'b' and 0 points for every 'a'.

40–50 points

It is extremely safe to say that you are quite a risk taker, almost to the extent that you may require many more lives than the proverbial cat if you wish to live to a ripe old age.

If nothing else, no one can accuse you of living a dull life, and many people must admire your courage and the lifestyle you lead. You are likely to be a person who has either made or lost a fortune, probably many times over, and will have many tales to tell about your exploits. Perhaps you should write your autobiography: it could well be a bestseller.

Seriously, though, it may be good advice just to curb your impulses slightly on occasions and remember the old adage of look before you leap. If you are able to do this then you are even more likely to be one of life's great successes, and live to a ripe old age into the bargain.

25–39 points

You are in the fortunate position of having found a happy medium in life. While not averse to taking the occasional risk, you do this in a measured, calculated way, having worked out all the options first.

Despite this, you still do derive some excitement from taking the occasional risk, providing this is not life threatening, and your life is all the richer for having done so.

Less than 25

You are the original steady Eddie who takes the sensible approach to life always, without ever finding the need to stick your neck out.

While this approach brings its rewards, don't forget that life is full of very rich experiences but sometimes we have to seek them out and take the occasional chance.

Doing something just for the hell of it can be a life enriching experience and it need not involve too much risk, and certainly need not present any danger to life or limb. So go on, be a devil, just occasionally!

Are you broadminded or prudish?

1 You are walking round an art gallery with your partner and are suddenly confronted by a 10 foot high statue of a male nude figure. What is your reaction?

   a) quite embarrassed
   b) not at all embarrassed, after all it is a beautiful work of art
   c) slightly embarrassed and we might make some humorous remark about its features

2 Do you think brothels should be legalised?

   a) no
   b) yes, as it would help to take prostitution off street corners
   c) perhaps, but I'm not too sure really

3 Do you disapprove of pornography?

   a) yes, very strongly
   b) I don't really disapprove of pornography
   c) I disapprove of certain kinds of pornography but not all

4 Would you ever bare all in a mixed sauna?

   a) no
   b) yes
   c) I might, but would initially be very nervous about
      doing so

5 Do you think TV soaps that are aired before the 9 p.m.
   watershed should tackle controversial issues such as gay
   marriages and underage teenage pregnancies?

   a) no, soaps, especially those which go out early
      evening, should be wholesome family entertainment
   b) yes, these are real-life issues which we should all face
      up to
   c) I am undecided but if they must be tackled it should
      be done with great care and delicacy

6 Do you ever tell dirty jokes?

   a) no way
   b) yes, often
   c) I admit I have done on rare occasions

7 Do you ever squirm with embarrassment when the
   conversation gets a little earthy in your company and
   sexual innuendoes start flying?

   a) yes, usually
   b) no
   c) yes, sometimes

8 Would you ever make a video recording of you and your
   partner making love?

a) no way
b) yes, how exciting
c) not sure, I would need some convincing on that one

9 If you were offered £25,000 to pose nude for a prestigious magazine, would you do it?

a) no
b) yes please
c) I would be sorely tempted, but am not sure I could go through with it

10 How often do you discuss love-making with your partner?

a) rarely or never
b) quite often
c) not very often

11 Your eldest daughter announces she is to become a top page three model. What is likely to be your reaction?

a) totally horrified and try to talk her out of it
b) feel pleased that you have such a beautiful daughter who has reached the height of her profession
c) feel somewhat shocked and upset, but tell her that if that is what she wants to do you will not stand in her way

12 Do four-letter swear words upset you?

a) yes
b) no, I don't mind and admit to using them myself on occasions
c) not upset me, but I don't like to hear them

13 You and your partner are watching television one evening and flick on to a channel which is showing a movie with a great deal of sexual content. What is likely to be your reaction?

a) quickly turn to another channel
b) continue watching and hope that it will put you and your partner in the mood for some similar passion
c) continue watching for a little while perhaps

14 Do you agree with the 9 o'clock watershed on television?

a) disagree as it should be later
b) disagree as it should be earlier
c) agree it is about right

15 Which offends you more on television, explicit sex or explicit violence?

a) explicit sex
b) explicit violence
c) both the same

16 You are at a party and someone has ordered a stripagram, not for yourself but for someone else. What is your reaction?

a) keep a very low profile quietly at the back of the room, or even slip out of the room altogether
b) get to the front of the room to get a good view of the action
c) just watch discreetly so as not to be seen as a party pooper, but try not to get involved in the action

17 You see your partner eyeing up a member of the opposite sex. Which one of the following is most likely to be your course of action?

  a) rebuke your partner
  b) turn a blind eye as it is something you do yourself quite often
  c) make a sarcastic comment such as 'have you seen enough?'

18 If you had the opportunity would you ever take part in an orgy?

  a) no
  b) yes
  c) maybe

19 Do you think any police action should be taken against streakers at sporting or public events?

  a) usually yes, they should be charged with some sort of offence such as breach of the peace or indecent behaviour
  b) no, surely it's just a bit of harmless fun
  c) it depends very much on the circumstances

20 Do you think there should be more sex shops?

  a) no
  b) yes, why not if there is the demand?
  c) maybe

21 Are you in favour of more censorship, or less?

  a) more
  b) less
  c) about the same as there is now

22 You are at a party and someone takes you to one side and starts to tell you an extremely risque joke. Which of the following is most likely to be your reaction?

 a) don't even let the person finish the joke, by making some form of excuse to move away or interrupting and changing the subject completely
 b) listen to the joke then tell an equally risque joke in return
 c) let your companion complete the joke but convey by some form of subtle body language that you were not impressed

23 Which one of the following is your favourite television comedy programme?

 a) Monty Python's Flying Circus
 b) The Benny Hill Show
 c) Frasier

24 Which of the following most accurately represents your views on the Internet?

 a) it doesn't interest me that much, especially as it is inundated with pornography
 b) it is an invaluable modern tool to have at one's disposal and a wonderful source for much valuable information
 c) it's OK as a learning tool and source of information

25 Were you embarrassed by answering any of the previous 24 questions in this test?

 a) yes, I found several of them very embarrassing
 b) not at all
 c) a little

Assessment

Award yourself 2 points for every 'a' answer, 0 points for every 'b', and 1 point for every 'c'.

40–50 points

Whether you realise it or not, your score indicates that you are an extremely prudish person, probably with high moral values.

While such values are highly commendable in modern society it may also be worth bearing in mind that there are two sides to every coin and standards set by one person about what is and what is not morally correct in society, and subsequently how society should conduct itself generally, are not necessarily the same as those that might be set by another person. In such cases it is very difficult to say who is right and who is wrong, if indeed it can be said that there is a right or wrong in such circumstances.

So while being correct to stick to your morals, even to the extent that you might become a campaigner against what you believe is wrong in our society, try to remember that each one of us has different desires and likes different things, and that just occasionally there is nothing wrong with having a little bit of fun, being a little bit naughty and spicing up your own life just a little.

25–39 points

You are a fairly broadminded person, and certainly not of a prudish nature.

While you have reasonably high moral values, you are likely to be a person who has, at the same time, an earthy sense of humour and is able to adapt to most situations. For example, if you are at a party you can conduct yourself in a dignified manner, but if the occasion demands it can trade risque jokes and innuendoes, and let your hair down with the best of them.

You are in the fortunate position of being able to enjoy the best of both worlds, and your life is likely to be much the richer for that.

Less than 25
Your score indicates that you are exceptionally broadminded with a good earthy sense of humour, and very much one of the lads or lasses.

You are in the fortunate position of being extremely open minded and not easily shocked, if indeed you are capable of being shocked at all.

The only word of caution to all this is never try to force your strong views and open-mindedness on others. Just remember that not everyone is so tolerant of the more open aspects of current society as you are, and you should have respect for these people and their views too. You may refer to these people as do-gooders and busybodies, but remember that they have as much right to their opinions as you have to yours, and as such you should have respect for these people and admire the courage they have in expressing their opinions, even though you may hold diametrically opposing views to them.

Are you anxious or relaxed?

1 Do you bite you fingernails?

   a) yes
   b) sometimes
   c) no

2 Do you ever find you cannot sleep because you have too much on your mind?

   a) yes, frequently
   b) sometimes
   c) only very occasionally

3 How often do you feel guilty about something you have done?

   a) quite often
   b) occasionally
   c) rarely or never

4 Do you tend to build things up in your mind more than you should do?

   a) yes, I do so often
   b) yes, occasionally
   c) sometimes, but not very often

5 Do you ever wake up with something worrying on your mind?

  a) yes
  b) only occasionally
  c) very rarely

6 How often do you completely relax and watch a movie on television?

  a) less than once every two weeks
  b) at least once a week on average
  c) more than once a week on average

7 When you take a holiday do you completely switch yourself off from your work?

  a) no, I am too busy to do so
  b) I try, but it is always there at the back of my mind
  c) yes

8 In general are you content with your lot in life

  a) not really
  b) I have to be, but things could be better
  c) yes

9 Do you ever take a long hot soak in the bath to relax yourself?

  a) no, I take a bath for the purpose of cleanliness only
  b) sometimes
  c) yes, a long soak in the bath is a great way to relax and unwind

10 When you get little aches and pains that you have not experienced before, do you tend to think it could be something serious?

a) yes, I worry until it goes away
b) sometimes
c) not really, but if it persisted I may go to see a doctor to have it checked out

11 Do you try to get a certain minimum number of hours sleep every night?

a) no, I'm too busy, the number of hours sleep I get each night, and my hours of sleep vary considerably
b) I try, but don't always succeed
c) yes, I usually make sure I get the minimum number of hours sleep each night that I believe I need to be refreshed the next day

12 One morning you decide to watch the finish of the cricket test match from Pakistan on television although you have lots of important work to do. Do you find yourself feeling guilty while watching the match that you are not doing your work?

a) yes, to a certain extent it spoils my enjoyment of watching the match
b) a little guilty perhaps, but I deserve the break and know I will catch up with my work later
c) no, it doesn't make me feel guilty

13 Have you ever considered taking some form of professional relaxation therapy such as acupuncture or aromatherapy?

a) yes

    b) no, but it could be something worth considering in
       the future
    c) no

14 How much does noise aggravate you?

    a) a great deal, in fact it sometimes sets my nerves right
       on edge
    b) sometimes it annoys me quite a bit
    c) occasionally, but generally it does not upset me a
       great deal

15 Do you often find yourself dashing around at more than
   your normal speed?

    a) yes, much of the time
    b) sometimes
    c) not very often

16 Does your throat ever tighten up in stressful situations?

    a) yes
    b) it has done on very rare occasions
    c) not that I have noticed

17 Does your job involve a lot of pressure such as working
   to tight deadlines?

    a) yes
    b) not a lot of the time, but it does occasionally
    c) no

18 How much do you think you laugh and smile compared
   to the average person?

    a) less

b) about the same

c) more

19 How often do you have one particular thing which dominates your thoughts for days on end?

a) quite often

b) just occasionally

c) very rarely or never

20 Are you optimistic about the future?

a) not particularly, as I worry about the future a great deal

b) neither optimistic nor pessimistic, whatever will be will be

c) yes, I am optimistic

21 Do you think it would be beneficial to take up yoga?

a) I think it might be a good idea if I had the time and patience

b) whatever for?

c) not particularly

22 Has anyone ever told you to relax more?

a) yes, many times

b) yes, on occasions

c) no

23 Have you ever suffered from any illness which has been diagnosed as stress related?

a) yes

b) no, but I am not so complacent as to say it would never happen

c) no

24 How often has your sex life suffered because you were stressed out?

a) more than occasionally
b) occasionally
c) never

25 How often do you feel yourself going red in the face because you are harassed rather than embarrassed?

a) more than occasionally
b) occasionally
c) very rarely or never

Assessment

Award yourself 2 points for every 'a' answer, 1 point for every 'b', and 0 points for every 'c'.

40–50 points

Your score indicates that you are of a somewhat overly anxious nature with a tendency to build many things up in your own mind out of all proportion. As this is in your nature, and likely to be the way in which you deal with things and cope with pressure, it is easier said than done to relax more and try not to worry about things so much.

It is worth remembering that anxiety does lead to stress and stress is the cause of many serious health problems. So if it is possible, do try to relax more and remember that the world does not revolve around you and that if you can just from time to time pause, take one step back and reflect on your life a little more, you are likely to feel much more at peace with the world and yourself, and find that life can be much more rewarding than you ever imagined it could be.

What you should try to do from time to time is switch off completely from your daily routine and relax completely for a few days lazing around the garden or listening to music and just generally chilling out. Then after this period of relaxation, do not dash straight back to the grindstone but instead spend some time doing something which you particularly enjoy such as shopping, having a few rounds of golf or straightening out the garden. This may also help you to get things into proportion so that when you do get back to the daily grind you may do so with a much more relaxed attitude and outlook.

25–39 points
You are in the fortunate position that although you do find yourself stressed out from time to time, this tends to be the exception rather than the norm, and you do recognise the warning signs that you are pushing yourself too far, and on these occasions are able to switch yourself off and slow yourself down a little.

Less than 25
You are one of those fortunate people whose attitude to life is extremely laid back and almost totally relaxed.

You do worry on occasions, as does every one of us, but you do tend to keep these occasions to the very minimum and for very short periods. Your attitude seems to be that by far the majority of things that we worry about in life never happen anyway, so there is no point in worrying about them until they actually do happen, which is very unlikely.

One word of caution, though: every one of us should be a little on our guard at times, and a relaxed attitude is fine, and indeed enviable, providing that you do not relax to the point of naivety.

How strong is your sense of justice?

1 What do you believe is the main purpose of imprisonment?

   a) to punish
   b) to protect the public
   c) to rehabilitate

2 If someone in high office is involved in a scandal which of the following do you believe should apply?

   a) they should resign immediately
   b) it depends on the circumstances and the people involved
   c) they need not necessarily resign as every one of us is allowed at least one mistake

3 Do you believe that people sentenced to life imprisonment for the most heinous crimes should end their lives in prison?

   a) yes
   b) yes, except in very exceptional circumstances
   c) not necessarily; there should be light at the end of the tunnel for every prisoner

4 Could you send someone to prison if you had the authority?

   a) yes
   b) maybe, but I would not feel happy about doing it
   c) no

5 How often do you join in an argument in favour of the underdog?

   a) very rarely, as the underdog is usually wrong
   b) occasionally if the underdog is someone I like or admire
   c) I usually do find myself siding with the underdog

6 You work in a shop and someone returns an unwanted gift. It is against the policy of the shop where you work to give refunds. How would you deal with such a situation?

   a) stick to your guns, reiterate the company policy to the customer, and tell them there is nothing you can do about it
   b) sympathise with the customer but tell them the company policy and suggest if they wish to take it further they write to the owner of the shop
   c) go to see the owner of the shop yourself and argue the customer's case

7 You discover that a colleague at work has been falsifying expense claims slightly. In which of the following ways are you most likely to deal with the situation?

   a) I would report my colleague to the management
   b) I would discuss it with other colleagues to see what they think should be done

c) warn my colleague that I know about the expense
    claim falsifying, and say that if it doesn't stop I will be
    forced to report the matter to the management

8 What do you think of the old adage that 'the punishment
   should fit the crime'?

   a) strongly agree
   b) generally agree, subject to taking into account the
       specific circumstances of each crime
   c) don't agree as you cannot make generalised
       statements of this nature. There are too many factors
       to take into account in each individual case

9 Do you believe in capital punishment?

   a) yes
   b) only in very exceptional circumstances
   c) no

10 Are you a stickler for the rules?

   a) yes
   b) usually, although there is no harm in bending the
       rules a little
   c) not particularly a stickler, and sometimes rules need
       to be reviewed and changed

11 What are your views on 'guilty beyond reasonable
    doubt'?

   a) it allows a lot of people to get away with it
   b) it allows everyone the right to a fair trial
   c) it is essential that in a free society that there should
       be such a high burden of proof

12 What are your views on people whose convictions are dismissed as unsafe after spending many years in prison?

   a) in most cases they probably did it anyway
   b) it is correct that these prisoners should be released as it is not certain they committed the crime for which they were originally convicted
   c) you feel very sad that a possibly innocent person has spent some of his or her life in prison

13 Do you think people in prison have it too soft?

   a) yes
   b) sometimes
   c) no, it's bad enough being deprived of your liberty without having to exist in harsh conditions

14 You see an elderly neighbour at the supermarket who absent-mindedly puts a packet of sweets in their pocket instead of their shopping basket. What would you do?

   a) I would have to report it to the manager
   b) as it was a neighbour I wouldn't do anything about it
   c) I would have a quiet word with them immediately and point out what they had done, and ask them if they were OK

15 Does injustice in other parts of the world worry you?

   a) no, other countries have a right to make their own laws and it is their business
   b) it doesn't worry me although I do recognise that such injustice exists
   c) yes

16 What do you think is the most important aspect of the European Human Rights Act?

   a) freedom of thought, conscience and religion
   b) freedom of assembly and association
   c) right to a fair trial

17 Which of the following most accurately represents your views on trade unions?

   a) I am not a great believer in trade unions
   b) they had far too much power in the 1960s. Thank goodness they are not so influential now
   c) they are absolutely necessary to protect and represent the rights of individuals in the workplace

18 What do you think of the Biblical expression 'an eye for an eye, a tooth for a tooth'?

   a) agree
   b) sometimes agree
   c) don't agree

19 Do you think we should ever temper punishment with mercy?

   a) very rarely if ever
   b) occasionally
   c) more than occasionally

20 Which of these movies is your favourite?

   a) 10 Rillington Place
   b) Rear Window
   c) Twelve Angry Men

21 Which of these most reflects your opinion of judges?

   a) fair

   b) too old

   c) out of touch

22 What do you think should be the place of politicians in the judicial process?

   a) to ensure the law is correctly interpreted

   b) to ensure sentencing is fair and appropriate

   c) to make the laws

23 The views of the victim should be sought before sentence is passed. What are your views on this?

   a) totally agree

   b) it would not serve any real purpose

   c) don't particularly agree

24 A close friend of yours is being tried for a crime. Which of the following most correctly describes your feelings about this?

   a) if he is guilty he should be prepared for his just deserts

   b) I hope he is found not guilty

   c) I hope he is proved to be innocent, but if found guilty he should be punished as anyone else would be

25 Would you ever break the law for a just cause?

   a) no

   b) I don't know

   c) yes

Assessment

Award yourself 2 points for every 'c' answer, 1 point for every 'b' and 0 points for every 'a'.

40–50 points

While you do have a strong sense of justice, this is moderated by an equally strong sense of fair play and a belief that society has a duty to continually strive to seek out the sources and reasons for crime and try to reform criminals whenever possible. While you believe in adequate punishment for a deserving criminal, you are not a believer in the old adage of 'lock him up and throw away the key'.

You find injustice deeply disturbing and as important to you as your desire to see criminals caught and punished.

This does not mean that you are a softy and tolerant of certain criminals within society. However, you do firmly believe that everyone has a right to a fair trial and to receive appropriate punishment, if found guilty. At the same time you have a great social conscience, and the need to get to the heart of society's problems is as important to you as the dispensing of justice and the need to see criminals get their just deserts.

25–39 points

You are certainly not a hard liner as far as justice is concerned, but you do believe that punishment should fit the crime and that justice for all is at the heart of our society. Nevertheless, a sense of justice is not, for you, the most emotive issue in life and, although important to you, it is not as important as many other issues which occupy your mind and thoughts.

You are a believer that in life we reap what we sow, that hard work will bring its rewards, that we in the main make our own luck and that natural justice will prevail.

Less than 25

Your results indicate that you also have a very strong sense of justice, and that you are in the main intolerant of transgressors within our society. You believe in tough sentencing and that the only way to achieve a decent and better society is for us all to uphold the law to the letter and continually strive towards stricter punishment for serious law breakers.

You are not convinced that serious criminals can be reformed and to a great extent are of the opinion that a leopard cannot change its spots.

The question of justice is to you one of the most important issues in life, and if you felt that you, yourself, had been dealt an injustice you would not rest until this had been remedied, and justice had been seen to be done.

Are you a leader or a follower?

1 What is the highest position you have ever attained during your working career?

   a) manager
   b) supervisor
   c) no supervisory or management position

2 Have you ever served on a committee?

   a) yes, as chair
   b) yes, as a committee member
   c) no

3 Do you think you would make a good politician?

   a) yes
   b) maybe
   c) no

4 To which of the following ambitions do you most aspire?

   a) to reach the very top of my profession
   b) to be financially secure
   c) to have a good and stable family life

5 Do you prefer to keep up to date with the latest fashions, or do your own individual thing?

   a) do my own thing
   b) a bit of both
   c) keep up with the latest fashions

6 What do you think about taking orders?

   a) not very happy
   ·b) it is sometimes necessary and I don't mind providing the orders are sensible and reasonable
   c) I don't mind at all

7 What style of work do you prefer?

   a) organising
   b) being left to my own devices
   c) being organised

8 A colleague with whom you have worked for many years on an equal footing is suddenly appointed to a position of seniority above you. Which of the following is most likely to be your reaction?

   a) quite upset and not sure if you can stomach it
   b) you wonder why it isn't you, but hope you can work with your colleague in the future and that it won't affect your friendship
   c) although disappointed it wasn't you, you don't reveal any negative feelings to your colleague, and offer your congratulations

9 When you first started work, did you expect that one day you would be the boss?

a) yes
b) I hoped I would be rather than expecting it
c) I didn't think about it that much

10 Have you ever organised anything in your community such as a Neighbourhood Watch scheme?

a) yes
b) no, but perhaps one day I might get more involved
c) no, I am happy to leave such things to others

11 Were you ever head boy or head girl at your school?

a) yes
b) no, but I was a prefect
c) no

12 Do you regard yourself as something of a trend setter?

a) yes
b) sometimes perhaps
c) not particularly

13 Would you leave a steady and secure job with no prospect of promotion, for a less secure job with similar pay, but with very high prospects of promotion?

a) yes
b) not sure what I would do unless the situation actually arose
c) no

14 Do you look up to people in authority?

a) no

b) sometimes
c) yes, usually

15 Do you believe that deep down we are all equals?

a) no
b) yes, although some are more equal than others
c) yes, I am a believer in a classless society

16 Do you believe in strong trade unions?

a) no
b) to a certain extent
c) yes

17 Have you ever organised a campaign against something you did not agree with or did not believe in?

a) yes
b) no, but I have participated in such a campaign
c) no

18 Which of the following politicians do you most admire?

a) Margaret Thatcher
b) Bill Clinton
c) Lech Walesa

19 Do you think strong leadership is necessary in the 21st century?

a) yes, there will always be a need for strong leadership
b) strong leadership is all well and good so long as we do not become a nanny state

c) no, strong leadership is an outmoded concept.
Cooperation between all is much more important
than strong leadership

20 Do people outside your immediate family ever turn to
you for advice?

a) yes, often
b) sometimes
c) never or rarely

21 Does the thought of being in power give you a kick?

a) yes
b) no
c) I have never even thought about it

22 You are in a restaurant with a group of friends where the
service is deplorable. After waiting for over one hour and
having made numerous complaints, which of the
following do you think is most likely to be your next
course of action?

a) suggest everyone abandons the evening and all walk
out in protest
b) sit there and complain and ask everyone else for their
opinion of what should be the next course of action
c) wait for someone to make a suggestion and go along
with the majority whatever they decide

23 Have you ever organised any sort of special get together
or reunion?

a) yes, on several occasions

b) yes, once
c) never

24 How sensitive are you to scathing criticism?

a) it is like water off a duck's back to me
b) I try not to let it bother me, although it can be hurtful on occasions
c) quite sensitive

25 Which of the following do you think is the most important leadership attribute?

a) charisma
b) motivation
c) experience

Assessment

Award yourself 2 points for every 'a' answer, 1 point for every 'b' and 0 points for every 'c'.

35–50 points

You exhibit great leadership qualities and this is what you aspire to, if indeed you have not reached the heights in your chosen career already.

If there is anything to organise you are only at your happiest if it is you doing the organising. You like to lead from the front, and be seen to be doing so, and find it frustrating to be in a situation where someone else is taking over the reins instead of yourself.

This is fine so long as you do not become impatient with people who might question you from time to time. Remember that no one is ever too old to learn, or change the way they do certain things from time to time, and often consultation is as much an important part of strong leadership as expecting people to follow your lead unquestioningly.

Keywords: ambition, drive, determination, resilience.

16–34 points

You exhibit good leadership qualities and like to be at the forefront of things, although to you this is not the most important thing in your life and you are happy to let someone else take over the reins providing you are consulted and agree with what they are doing, and the way they are doing it.

Keywords: conscientious, team-player, patient, philosophical.

Below 16

It appears that you do not aspire to be a leader and are happier for others to take the initiative.

This is fine for you and although it is unlikely that you will reach the dizziest heights of leadership due to your lack of ambition, your hard work and graft could bring you some unexpected promotion from time to time.

To a great extent you may lack confidence in your own ability and do not wish to be seen as someone who likes to push themselves continually forward. You are the traditional grafter, happy with your lot, and the niche in life you have created for yourself.

Keywords: content, hard-working, unambitious, unselfish.

Creativity

The term *creativity* refers to mental processes that lead to solutions, ideas, concepts, artistic forms, theories or products that are unique and novel.

The creative functions are controlled by the right-hand hemisphere of the human brain. This is the side of the brain which is under-used by the majority of people, as opposed to the thought processes of the left-hand hemisphere, which is characterised by order, sequence and logic, and is responsible for such functions as numerical and verbal skills.

Because it is under-used, much creative talent in many people remains untapped throughout life. Until we try, most of us never know what we can actually achieve. We know that we all have a creative side to our brain, therefore we all have the potential to be creative. However, because of the pressures of modern living and the need for specialisation, many of us never have the time or opportunity, or indeed are given the encouragement, to explore our latent talents, even though most of us have sufficient ammunition to realise this potential in the form of data which has been fed into, collated and processed by the brain over many years.

Because it is such a diverse subject, and because in so many people it is to a great extent unexplored, creativity is very difficult to measure.

The following three different types of exercises are all designed with the object of improving or recognising your own powers of creativity and generation of ideas and artistic skill.

Exercise one

In each of the following use your imagination to create an original sketch or drawing of something recognisable incorporating the symbol already provided.

You have 30 minutes in which to complete the twelve drawings.

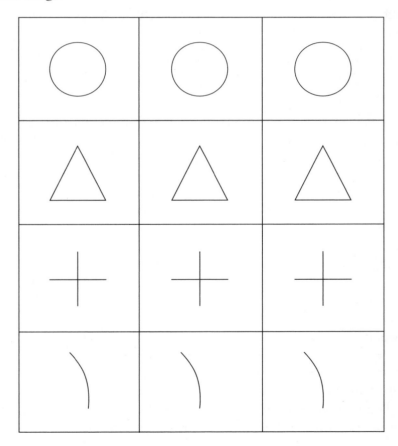

Analysis

You can mark this test yourself, but it is best marked by a friend or family member.

Award one mark for each recognisable sketch, providing it is not similar to any of the other sketches.

For example, if you draw a face, a second face scores no point as each sketch must have an original theme.

You thus obtain marks for variety. If you are creative you will tend to try to draw something different for each sketch.

There is no correct answer to each of the twelve sketches, because for each there is an infinite number of ideas.

Scoring:

11–12 points	exceedingly creative
7–10 points	very creative
4–6 points	average

Repeat the exercise as many times as you wish. Try other geometric objects or lines as a starting point

Exercise two

The object here is to interpret each of the twelve drawings in the wildest and most imaginative way you can.

You may also try playing the game with other people. The more wild you think someone's suggestion, the better it is and the more creative they are. For example, you might think that drawing number 1 is the tip of a pool or snooker cue. But is there anything else it can be? Let your imagination run riot and see what you can come up with.

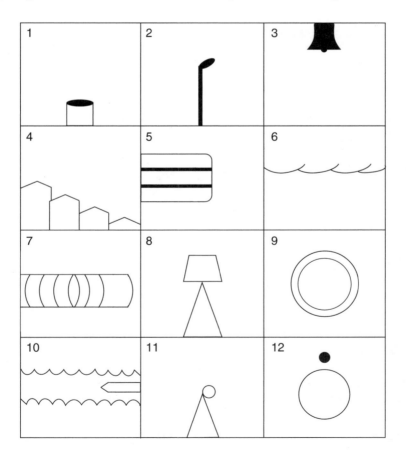

Exercise three

This test is based on Gestalt and Jackson's Test of Divergent Ability, which requires the subject to name as many new uses as possible for an everyday object such as a brick or a piece of string.

Here, you are required to name up to 12 new uses for a bucket in 10 minutes. You should work strictly to the time limit otherwise your score will be invalidated.

1 ....

2 ....

3 ....

4 ....

5 ....

6 ....

7 ....

8 ....

9 ....

10 ....

11 ....

12 ....

Scoring and analysis
You can mark your efforts yourself, but it is better if you get a friend or family member to do so.

Allow:
2 points for any good or original answer
1 point for a good attempt
0 points for completely impractical answers

Scoring:
18–24 points   highly creative
13–17 points   above average
 7–12 points   average

Now try the same again but this time think up uses for a paper clip:

1 ....

2 ....

3 ....

4 ....

5 ....

6 ....

7 ....

8 ....

9 ....

10 ....

11 ....

12 ....

Now repeat the exercise as many times as you wish with other common household objects such as a comb, a rubber band or an empty milk bottle.

Are you in the right job?

Choose just the one alternative that most applies to you in each of the 25 questions.

1 Why do you go to work?

   a) for money
   b) for money and for something to do
   c) for job satisfaction and money

2 How often do you apply for new jobs either within or outside the organisation for which you are working?

   a) more than twice a year
   b) twice a year
   c) less than twice a year

3 Which of these best describes your work philosophy?

   a) it's part of life's drudgery
   b) it's a living
   c) it should be fun

4 How do you relate to your working colleagues?
   a) I cannot stand them
   b) I get on so-so with them
   c) they are my friends and colleagues

5 At the end of your normal working day you have an ongoing job which is not quite finished. What do you do?

   a) go home, and finish the job the morning after
   b) finish the job but claim overtime
   c) finish the job whether or not you are paid overtime

6 How do you relate to your boss?

   a) not very well
   b) satisfactorily
   c) I am the boss

7 You wake up on a Monday morning after a week's holiday. What do you think?

   a) I've been dreading this day all week
   b) ah well, back to the grindstone
   c) I'll get in early this morning to catch up on what has been happening last week

8 How do you rate your work content?

   a) very mundane
   b) it could be more interesting or varied
   c) I enjoy what I do

9 After a day's work how do you feel?

   a) glad it's over for another day
   b) exhausted, either physically or mentally
   c) satisfied

10 You glance at your watch and it's 3 p.m. Just two hours to go. What do you think?

a) it's going to be a long two hours
b) how am I going to get everything done by 5 p.m.?
c) it's soon got to 3 p.m.

11 How often do you find yourself getting wound up at work?

a) almost every day
b) more than once a week
c) very rarely

12 How often do you self-certify yourself sick and unable to attend work?

a) more than five days a year
b) less than five days a year
c) less than two days a year

13 Late on a Sunday afternoon do you ever feel depressed about going back to work the day after?

a) yes, frequently
b) sometimes
c) I never feel depressed about going back to work the following day

14 How often do you look at the office or works clock, or glance at your wristwatch during the course of a working day?

a) at least once an hour
b) probably two or three times a day
c) just occasionally

15 What worries you most about work?

   a) job security
   b) having too much to do
   c) being totally competent and professional

16 What is your attitude to new technology?

   a) I don't want anything to do with it if it can possibly be avoided
   b) I have to accept it, but I do worry if I can be flexible enough to adapt to it
   c) I welcome it as an exciting new challenge

17 You are asked to go on a training course. What do you say?

   a) I don't really fancy this. Leave me out if possible
   b) OK, but I'm really much too busy to attend
   c) I welcome it, if it is relevant to the job I am doing

18 How wide an interest do you take in the organisation in which you are working?

   a) not all that much; I'm there to do the job I do
   b) I'm aware of what is going on, but my main preoccupation is with the job I do
   c) I do take a wide interest in the organisation in which I work

19 How often do you have a laugh with your colleagues?

   a) not very often
   b) sometimes
   c) quite often

20 Do you ever daydream at work?

   a) yes, often
   b) I haven't time to daydream
   c) occasionally

21 You are asked to write an article for the works
    newspaper on your hobby. How would you respond?

   a) write the article in working hours and think this was a
      nice break from your usual job
   b) ask if you could do the article in paid overtime
   c) write the article in your own time

22 Your official time for starting work each morning is 8.30.
    If you got into work at 8.10, for example, what would
    you do?

   a) wonder what had gone wrong with your time-keeping
   b) read your newspaper until 8.30
   c) start work as soon as you got in

23 How often do you attend works social functions?

   a) never
   b) just occasionally
   c) fairly often

24 If it was suddenly announced that your place of work is
    moving to another part of the country and you are to be
    given the alternative of moving or redundancy, what
    would be your immediate reaction?

   a) not particularly worried, I would take the redundancy
      and look for another job

b) I would be quite upset and know that I had a very
difficult decision to make

c) I would want to relocate with the job if at all possible

25 How often do you have working lunches?
a) never
b) always
c) sometimes

Assessment

Award yourself 2 points for every 'c' answer, 1 point for
every 'b' and 0 points for every 'a'.

40–50 points
You are in the fortunate position of doing the job you love in
exactly the right environment. For you Monday mornings
present no problems – you are actually looking forward to
the day ahead and any new challenges with a relish that
must sometimes be the envy of your colleagues. And because
you are so content in your working life, this reflects on your
personal life too, making your whole existence less stressful.
Unless there is a real pressing need to improve yourself
because of, for example, financial reasons you have no need
for change in your working life.

25–39 points
As far as job satisfaction is concerned you are Mr/Ms Average.
Sometimes you enjoy your job immensely, but sometimes
you become disillusioned, or even hate it. At the end of the
day it's just a job as far as you are concerned and you
probably wouldn't bother going out to work at all if it wasn't
for the money. You really look forward to your holidays and
weekends, and winning the lottery, but often say to yourself

that things could be a lot worse. You should make the most of the aspects of your work that you really do enjoy and think about how you can improve the other, less agreeable, parts. As to finding another, more enjoyable job, there is no harm in exploring the possibilities of a change of career, but don't jump into things feet first just for the sake of it. Remember, it's sometimes better the devil you know!

Less than 25

Try to work at changing the job you are doing for the better, either in conjunction with your boss or with your colleagues. If this is not possible then you should seriously look towards a change of job, either within the organisation where you work or a complete career change altogether. At present you are unhappy in your present job and this may even spill over into your private life and affect your friends and family. Change, however, can sometimes take courage. It's your choice.

Are you a saint or a sinner?

1 What is your opinion of the old adage 'charity begins at home'?

   a) disagree
   b) yes, if needs must
   c) agree

2 Would you ever have an extra-marital affair, or always remain faithful to your partner?

   a) remain faithful
   b) don't know
   c) have an affair

3 Do you live to eat, or eat to live?

   a) eat to live
   b) both
   c) live to eat

4 Have you ever jumped the queue?

   a) no
   b) yes, but only very occasionally
   c) yes, more than occasionally

5 A colleague of yours wins £3 million on the National Lottery. What is your reaction?

   a) you are genuinely pleased for your colleague
   b) pleased for your colleague, but think if only I could have luck like that
   c) what a lucky swine! Why couldn't it have been me?

6 If you couldn't control your anger would you ever think of seeking therapy to do something about it?

   a) yes
   b) no, I would try to deal with it myself. Having recognised there was a problem I believe I could take my own steps to deal with it
   c) no

7 You are a single person and your best friend starts dating a partner to whom you find yourself extremely attracted. Which of the following is likely to be your reaction to this situation?

   a) keep my feelings to myself for as long as the relationship between my friend and this person continues
   b) keep my feelings to myself but attempt a bit of subtle flirting with my friend's partner to see if I can detect any spark of feelings for me
   c) as a first step make sure my friend's partner knows my feelings for them and give them every chance to reciprocate their feelings for me

8 What is your reaction to the old adage 'enough is as good as a feast'?

a) agree, I only eat as much as I need to satisfy my appetite
b) agree, but it is impolite to leave uneaten food on your plate
c) disagree, give me a feast any time

9 Do you ever wish you had the Wisdom of Solomon?

a) it is certainly something to aspire to
b) yes
c) never thought about it

10 What do you think about people who boast about their achievements?

a) they are insecure and worry that people may think they are inadequate
b) it doesn't bother me
c) it annoys me

11 Do you believe in the triumph of good over evil?

a) yes
b) not sure
c) not in this day and age

12 Do you consider yourself to be the eternal optimist?

a) yes
b) not the eternal optimist, although I am an optimist to a certain extent
c) no, I would have to describe myself as more of a pessimist than an optimist

13 How much do you have to motivate yourself to carry out mundane tasks?

   a) a little, but if they have to be done, they have to be done
   b) quite a lot
   c) a great deal, and if I can avoid doing them, or delegate them, I will

14 Do you try to 'keep up with the Jones's'?

   a) no
   b) no, in fact I don't even want to know the Jones's
   c) yes, if possible

15 How often have you donated to a television appeal?

   a) many times
   b) occasionally
   c) never

16 Which of the following describes your religious beliefs?

   a) I believe in God
   b) agnostic
   c) atheist

17 How often have you been so drunk you could not walk in a straight line?

   a) never
   b) less than five times
   c) five times or more

18 Should reformed perpetrators of very serious crime ever
    be accepted back into society?

    a) yes, if they have served their time and been reformed
       that is a great achievement for both them and society
       and we should accept them back unequivocally
    b) maybe, but only in very exceptional circumstances
    c) there are certain criminals we should never allow
       back into society and I do not believe they can ever
       be reformed completely

19 Which of the following do you most admire?

    a) triumph over adversity
    b) an act of great courage
    c) a rags to riches story

20 Do you regard cigarettes as a kind of drug?

    a) yes
    b) not sure
    c) no

21 Do you believe in legalising soft drugs?

    a) no
    b) perhaps
    c) yes

22 Do you think there is any harm in gambling?

    a) yes
    b) only when it becomes more than just a bit of fun
    c) no, if people want to gamble that is their business

23 How much television do you watch on average every day, if by watching television that means not doing anything else at the same time?

   a) less than two hours
   b) more than two hours but less than four hours
   c) more than four hours

24 Do you find people who rattle collection boxes under your nose in supermarkets annoying?

   a) no
   b) sometimes
   c) yes

25 Does it ever worry you that when you occasionally live the high life that there are starving millions in the world?

   a) yes
   b) no, but perhaps it should
   c) no

Assessment

Award yourself 2 points for every 'a' answer, 1 point for every 'b', and 0 points for every 'c'.

The seven deadly sins	*The seven virtues*
sloth	charity
anger	faith
covetousness	fortitude
envy	hope
gluttony	justice
lust	prudence
pride	temperance

40–50 points
You are definitely a saint of very high moral values, and the original Good Samaritan.

The problem is, of course, and you probably know this already, the difficulty and pressure which you have put on yourself in maintaining the very high standards that you have set, and this may sometimes be a worry to you.

The main thing to remember is that everyone is different and that it does not suit everyone to live their life to the same standard, and that someone who has different standards to yourself is not necessarily wrong. Tolerance is also an important virtue, as is the philosophy of live and let live.

25–39 points
You are neither saint nor sinner, and to a great extent live your life in the middle lane of knowing what is right and what is wrong, while still not being averse to letting your hair down from time to time and being a little adventurous and hedonistic.

Rest assured that everyone of us is a saint in some respects and a sinner in others; it's just that some of us are more saint than sinner and others more sinner than saint.

Less than 25
You are definitely a sinner who has let your halo slip, if indeed you ever had one.

This, however, does not necessarily make you a bad person. At least you do not lack honesty, otherwise you would have answered the above questions differently and obtained a score which would have put you in the middle bracket.

While you probably think you enjoy life to the full, it may be to your advantage on occasions to have a little more humility and appreciate that there are people not quite so fortunate as yourself who need more than just a little of our help.

Do you look on the bright side?

1 What are your feelings at the end of a very enjoyable holiday?

   a) upset and some feeling of depression that it's over
   b) looking forward to the next holiday
   c) you feel refreshed and you're looking forward to getting home and catching up with all the news

2 It's your fortieth birthday. What are your feelings?

   a) the best years of my life are over
   b) I'm getting older but I'll just have to make the best of things
   c) life begins at forty

3 You have been in perfect health for the past ten years. What are your thoughts about this?

   a) it can't last
   b) I've been lucky for the past ten years; let's hope I'm as lucky for the next ten
   c) I will work at keeping myself in good shape so that I will have a better chance of staying in good health in the future

4 You are going through one of life's bad patches. What is your philosophy on this?

   a) I seem to have more than my share of bad patches
   b) life's a bitch
   c) life can be a bitch at times but these bad times won't last forever

5 You have just been made redundant without any warning. What is your reaction?

   a) you feel like it's the end of the world
   b) you are upset and hope you can find another job quickly
   c) you are upset but think that it may give you the opportunity for change which may in the long run be for the best

6 You have a gamble on the Grand National. What are your expectations?

   a) your horse will probably fall at the first fence
   b) you don't really expect to win but hope you get a good run for your money
   c) you work out your anticipated winnings even before the race has started

7 What would be your thoughts if someone said 'life is not a rehearsal'?

   a) it would have turned out a lot better than this if I had been able to rehearse it
   b) I don't agree, there is something better after this life
   c) it's a good job I am making the best of things then

8 What is your attitude to taking chances?

   a) I don't take any chances if it can be avoided
   b) I think it is necessary to take chances from time to time
   c) I like taking chances, it gives me a buzz

9 Why do you take part in sport?

   a) for something to do
   b) I like competing and I like the friendships that can be forged
   c) to win

10 What do you think if a decision goes against you that you can't reverse?

   a) quite put out about it
   b) try to see the other point of view
   c) think that perhaps it might be for the best in the long run

11 You have come to the end of a relationship that really you would like to continue even though you accept it is not possible. What are your feelings?

   a) devastated
   b) that you will get over it one day but it will take a long time
   c) I must try to put this behind me quickly and get on with the rest of my life

12 What is your attitude to change?

   a) change is never for the better
   b) change, like death and taxes, is inevitable
   c) it's a whole new challenge

13 You are told that a giant meteor will strike earth in 10 minutes and there is very little chance anyone will survive. What is your reaction?

   a) I've got to die sometime, it might as well be now
   b) find your loved one to say your goodbyes
   c) someone always survives. Now what can I do to increase the chances of it being me?

14 You come to one of life's many crossroads and don't know which way to turn. What do you think?

   a) whatever I do it will probably be wrong
   b) I wish I could go back instead of forward
   c) fate will decide, and whichever route I choose it will turn out for the best

15 You are going through a bad patch in a relationship. How do you feel?

   a) it looks like this is the end of this relationship
   b) things are getting from bad to worse
   c) we will work things out

16 You and your partner seem to be developing different interests. How do you feel?

   a) that you seem to be growing apart

b) you accept the inevitability of what is happening but wish you could share everything together as you once did

c) you are pleased for your partner and feel that the different interests are all part of you both growing as individuals

17 What are your feelings about autumn?

a) slightly depressed that it will soon be winter

b) no particular feelings, it's just another time of the year

c) it is a beautiful time of the year

18 What do you think when you get the odd ache or pain?

a) I tend to worry it might be something serious

b) I hope it will soon disappear but think that if it doesn't I will pay a visit to the doctor to be on the safe side

c) I don't think too much about it. Little aches and pains come and go all the time

19 What is your reaction when someone talks about the 'good old days'?

a) I agree, things were better in years gone by

b) there were good times in the past as there will be again

c) generally, things are getting better, we have a lot of exciting time to look forward to

20 How much of a part do you think luck plays in one's life?

a) a great deal
b) some people are luckier than others
c) to a great extent you make your own luck

21 Imagine yourself in a dangerous life-threatening situation like the characters trapped on the top floor in the movie 'The Towering Inferno'. What are your thoughts?

a) this is it, I'm going to die
b) how on earth did I get into this situation? It's like a bad dream
c) when I get out of this I'll celebrate

22 You have just been dealt one of life's bitter disappointments. What is your reaction?

a) it always happens to me
b) you feel as though you have been kicked in the stomach
c) win some, lose some

23 You go out for a meal with friends and it turns out to be a disaster. You wait two hours to be served, the sprouts are hard and all the food is cold. What is your reaction?

a) every time I go out to enjoy myself something seems to go wrong
b) you and your friends come to the conclusion that you can't do anything about it as it's just typical in this day and age
c) you have a good laugh about it, but write to the restaurant to complain and hope you will be invited back for a free meal

24 You have a sudden windfall of £5,000. What is your reaction?

    a) £5,000 isn't going to get me very far these days
    b) I'm going to treat myself to some little luxury I haven't quite been able to afford up to now
    c) good luck always comes in threes, another two to go

25 Your car skids out of control and ends up in a ditch upside down but you scramble out unscathed. What is your immediate reaction?

    a) oh no, look at my car, it's a write-off
    b) this is bad luck, all that hassle with the insurance, and how long am I going to be without a car?
    c) I'm lucky to be alive

Assessment

Award yourself 2 points for every 'c' answer, 1 point for every 'b' and 0 points for every 'a'.

40–50 points

What a wonderful outlook on life you have! Not for you the sleepless nights worrying about things that may never happen. You are the eternal optimist who always looks on the bright side whatever happens and firmly believes that every cloud has a silver lining. As long as you do not tend to become naive about life's sometimes harsh realities, then you are the envy of us all, carefree, but at the same time knowing that you can get the best out of life as long as you are prepared to accept the downs with the ups.

20–39 points

Like the majority of people in this world, you are a realist.
You know that life is a roller coaster but hopefully the high
points will exceed the down points and this is what really
counts in the end. While you do not consider yourself to be
a pessimist, perhaps you can learn a little from the eternal
optimist and try not to worry so much. Remember that most
of the things that we do worry about in life never happen
anyway. Why worry about anything unless it actually does
happen?

Less than 20 points

You are a born pessimist. While this doesn't make you a
worse person externally, and you can still be successful and
have many friends, it does mean that you suffer from a great
deal of inner turmoil and you are constantly nagged by
doubts and worries about almost everything. What you must
try not to do is make mountains out of molehills. Instead try
to put negative thoughts to the back of your mind. Try to
think of the positive side of life. There are many people in a
worse position than yourself. If you can do this, and it may
take a great deal of effort on your part to achieve, you will
start to feel the benefits, both health-wise and by an
improved outlook on life in general.

How aggressive are you?

In general, aggression is a form of animal behaviour characterised by an assault or attack on one animal by another This can take the form of conflict between members of different species for the purpose of obtaining food or defence, or attacks directed towards members of the same species, for example, in the way that goats butt their heads together.

In humans, the term *aggression* is a general term used for a wide variety of acts including attack or hostility towards one another, and this can be caused by such factors as fear or frustration, a desire to produce fear or flight in others and a tendency to invoke one's ideas or interests on others.

In humans learned experience is important in determining the level of aggressive behaviour, and generally the trading of insults or the presence of weapons have all been learned from various sources.

The obtaining of rewards by children, such as toys, attention and sweets, as a result of aggressive behaviour, is also likely to reinforce such behaviour. Children also learn aggression by observing others, by having role models and by the influence of the mass media.

In general, the kind of aggression that most people tend to think of when the term is used is aggression evoked by frustration or the thwarting of one's goals. It is also typified by a display of the will to power and the desire to control others.

1 You want something in life really badly. Which of the following most accurately describes your attitude to this?

   a) hope I will get it, but don't build my hopes up too much until I do
   b) try very hard to get what I want
   c) not rest until I get what I want

2 Have you ever shouted at someone over the telephone who is being unhelpful or obstructive?

   a) no, shouting at people is not my style
   b) not shout, but on rare occasions I have raised my voice or adapted an angry or impatient tone
   c) yes

3 Do you believe that 'attack is the best form of defence'?

   a) not really
   b) perhaps in certain situations
   c) yes

4 How often do you lose your temper?

   a) less than three times a year
   b) between three and six times a year
   c) more than six times a year

5 You learn to your horror that a major building programme is to take place in a wooded area at the back of your home, which will mean the destruction of some 50 mature trees. You are totally opposed to the scheme. Which of the following is most likely to be your course of action?

   a) probably do nothing, except complain privately to my friends, neighbours and family, as what has already been decided will go ahead anyway

  b) write a formal letter of objection to the planning
     department of your local council.
  c) organise your neighbours into some sort of protest
     committee

6 How often do you analyse or question your own conduct
  or your reactions to certain situations?

  a) frequently
  b) sometimes
  c) never or very rarely

7 You are driving your car and another driver almost
  causes you to be involved in an accident. Do you:

  a) shrug your shoulders and consider yourself lucky the
     accident never happened
  b) have a good moan about the other driver to yourself
     or to your car passenger
  c) gesticulate angrily to the other driver with, perhaps, a
     few choice words

8 Do you think aggressive behaviour is necessary as a
  means to an end?

  a) not really, but if it is, then it isn't my style
  b) in certain circumstances it may be necessary
  c) yes

9 How often do you use mild expletives?

  a) never or rarely
  b) fairly often
  c) very often

10 Have you ever resorted to violence?

   a) no, and I cannot ever foresee any circumstance where
       I would
   b) no, but I cannot rule out the possibility that in certain
       very exceptional circumstances I might
   c) yes

11 What is your reaction to the statement 'wars start when
   evil triumphs over good'?

   a) agree
   b) not sure
   c) don't necessarily agree

12 Someone does you a particularly bad turn. Which of the
   following is most likely to be your reaction?

   a) do nothing except put it down to experience and
       make a mental note never to trust that person again
   b) have a quiet word with them in private and ask them
       why they did it
   c) not rest until you can get one back on them

13 Do you think you have a ruthless streak?

   a) no
   b) maybe
   c) yes

14 Have you ever vented your frustration on a store clerk
   who is being particularly negative and unhelpful?

   a) no, that sort of attitude doesn't get you anywhere
   b) very occasionally
   c) yes, more than occasionally

15 For the third Saturday night in a row your new
    neighbours in the adjoining house are holding an all-
    night noisy party. Which of the following is most likely to
    be your course of action?

    a) have a very quiet word with them during the
        following week to ask them if it is possible to keep
        the noise down in future, as you are losing sleep
    b) contact the local council to enquire if it is possible to
        take formal action to force them to reduce the noise
        level
    c) bang on the adjoining wall when the noise is at its
        height

16 Have you ever become so angry that you have shaken
    your fist at someone?

    a) no
    b) no, but I cannot rule out the possibility that I may
        one day under certain circumstances
    c) yes

17 You are faced with a choice of three documentaries on
    television one evening. Which one would you choose?

    a) wildlife in Alaska
    b) the era of prohibition in America
    c) the Japanese bombing of Pearl Harbour

18 How often do you use very strong expletives?

    a) never
    b) very occasionally
    c) more than occasionally

19 What are your views on people who thump the table at meetings?

   a) seems childish
   b) in almost all cases it will not help them to get their own way
   c) sometimes such actions are necessary to get your point across and convince others

20 Which one of these is your favourite sport on television?

   a) bowls
   b) snooker
   c) boxing

21 Which one of these is your favourite type of comedy?

   a) situation comedy
   b) farce
   c) satire

22 You put some money into a machine at a car park to obtain a ticket and nothing happens. Which of these is most likely to be your initial reaction?

   a) press a few buttons then put some more money in to see if it works this time
   b) try to seek out the car park attendant to explain what has happened
   c) thump the machine

23 Are you a bad or a good loser?

   a) good
   b) there is no such thing as a good loser, it's just that some show it more than others.
   c) bad

24 Have you ever cheated to win at anything?

    a) no
    b) perhaps bent the rules a little
    c) yes

25 Which of these sums up your feelings towards scenes of violence in the movies?

    a) it is much better, and just as effective, when violence is suggested rather than shown in graphic detail
    b) I don't like such scenes, but they do occur and, therefore, should be shown. After all, art is life and life is art
    c) why not show things if they actually do occur? After all, they can be quite exciting and give people something of a kick

Assessment

Award yourself 2 points for every 'a' answer, 1 point for every 'b', and 0 points for every 'c'.

40–50 points

Your score indicates that you are of an extremely passive nature.

    While this means that you are likely to go through life without upsetting anyone and are likely to make many friends, it may also mean that you are likely to be put upon, and in certain circumstances bullied. It may be necessary to try to toughen up just a little, while still retaining your charm and placid nature, if you are to realise many of your ambitions and aspirations.

25–39 points

While you are generally of a passive nature, you are able to call on a degree of measured aggression just at the right time when it is necessary.

While knowing what you want out of life you have just the correct temperament to enable you to achieve this without walking over everyone else in order to fulfil your ambitions.

Less than 25

You appear at times to be somewhat dominated by your aggressive nature.

You should attempt to analyse your behaviour patterns and your reactions to certain situations to see if there are other ways of achieving your aspirations by, for example, diplomacy rather than demand.

It may also assist you considerably if you can devote more time to some form of creative or recreational therapeutical pursuit or hobby, such as painting, writing or gardening.

Are you a night person?

1 What time do you usually get out of bed on a Sunday morning?

   a) before 8 a.m.
   b) between 8 a.m. and 9.30 a.m.
   c) after 9.30 a.m.

2 When is a big city at its most attractive?

   a) early morning, when the sun is rising and there are very few people about
   b) during the day when it is full of the bustle of shoppers
   c) after dark

3 What do you prefer to watch on television?

   a) a daytime soap
   b) the mid-evening news
   c) a midnight movie

4 You are going out for an evening meal with friends. What time of the evening would you prefer to book the meal?

   a) before 8 p.m.
   b) between 8 p.m. and 9 p.m.
   c) After 9 p.m.

5 It's 3 a.m. and you are in bed but cannot get to sleep.
What do you do?

   a) just lie there and try hard to go to sleep
   b) start counting sheep
   c) get up and read a book or watch some television

6 What time on average do you go to bed?

   a) before 11 p.m.
   b) before midnight
   c) after midnight

7 When do you feel at your most creative?

   a) when you wake up on a morning fully revived from a
      good night's sleep
   b) between 10 a.m. and 2 p.m.
   c) late at night

8 After a holiday in New York what would be likely to be
your most vivid and lasting memory?

   a) a boat trip round the Statue of Liberty
   b) a visit to Macey's department store
   c) the lights of Broadway

9 If you were invited to an evening out of your choice,
which would you choose?

   a) a VIP seat at a sporting event such as a top premier
      league football match
   b) a meal followed by a seat at a top West End theatre
   c) a late night cabaret and meal

10 How much sleep do you require each night?

    a) four hours solid will suffice
    b) more than four but less than seven hours
    c) more than seven hours

11 Do you ever burn the midnight oil when you have lots of work to do?

    a) never
    b) very rarely
    c) sometimes

12 How often do you feel drowsy during the day yet wide awake at night?

    a) very rarely
    b) sometimes
    c) frequently

13 Which of these is the most romantic situation?

    a) a picnic by the lake on a hot summer's afternoon
    b) a visit to the cinema
    c) a moonlight stroll along the beach at midnight on a balmy summer's night

14 What do you eat for breakfast when staying at a hotel on holiday?

    a) a full English breakfast in the dining room
    b) continental breakfast in your room
    c) you are usually so crashed out from the night before that you miss breakfast

15 It's Friday and you have finished work for the weekend.
    What would you prefer to do?

    a) stay in for the evening and unwind
    b) go down the pub or club until closing time
    c) go clubbing until the early hours

16 Your partner offers to buy you clothes for your birthday.
    What would you choose?

    a) some new work clothes
    b) sports clothes
    c) evening wear

17 When do you prefer to have long phone conversations
    with friends?

    a) during the day
    b) after 6 p.m. when it is cheap rate
    c) late at night when I am completely unwound

18 Do you like driving at night?

    a) not particularly
    b) I have no particular preference whether I drive at
        night or during the day
    c) yes

19 Which of these sounds appeals to you most?

    a) the dawn chorus of birds
    b) a Salvation Army band on a Sunday morning
    c) mellow music on the radio

20 What is your favourite colour?

   a) pink
   b) yellow
   c) blue

21 If you could adopt a second lifestyle, which of these would appeal to you most?

   a) an athlete
   b) an actor
   c) a singer

22 Which of these is your favourite food?

   a) bacon and eggs
   b) a roast
   c) oysters

23 How often do you fall asleep before you go to bed at night?

   a) rarely
   b) sometimes
   c) often

24 When do you usually go to bed?

   a) earlier than your partner
   b) at the same time as your partner
   c) later than your partner

25 If you were given the choice of spending some money on your house, which of the following would you choose?

a) new garden furniture
b) new dining room furniture
c) new light fittings

Assessment

Award yourself 2 points for every 'c' answer, 1 point for every 'b' and 0 points for every 'a'.

35–50 points
You are most definitely a night person, the original night-owl. You probably start to flag at times of the day when most people are at their peak and start to come into your own at a time when most people are thinking of turning in for a good night's sleep. For you early mornings when the alarm goes off must seem like a bad dream and you cannot believe it is that time of the day already – if only it was the weekend and you could have a lie-in. Just remember, though, the old adage about burning the candle at both ends. Just occasionally why not treat yourself to an early night just to try and catch up a little, although on such evenings you will probably wake up in the early hours and finish up creeping downstairs to raid the refrigerator. Also try to catch forty winks during the day. It is surprising, but sometimes a two or three minute 'power nap' can do you the world of good.

16–34 points
While you might from time to time let your hair down and have the occasional late night you are by no means a night-owl. You are Mr/Ms Average in that you do not do things by excesses. You need between six and eight hours sleep a night to be at your best, and once you get to sleep you would expect that to be it until the alarm goes off in the morning.

Below 16

To you a good night's sleep is essential for you to be at your best during the day, which for you is the time that matters most and when you can devote your energies to your career and/or your family, in other words the things that matter most to you. You love the early mornings, especially in spring or summer when the birds are singing and the sun is shining through a chink in the curtains when you waken up, and you are probably a fitness fanatic who either goes for an early morning jog or does their exercises then jumps in the shower before getting ready for work wide awake and fully refreshed for the day ahead. The old adage 'early to bed, early to rise, makes a man healthy, wealthy and wise' could almost have been written just for you.

Are you a shrinking violet?

Choose the one alternative that most applies to you in each of the 25 questions.

1 When do you feel most relaxed?

   a) in your own company
   b) with two or three family and friends
   c) at a fairly large social gathering

2 At a social function you are in a group of four or five people. How do you usually behave?

   a) do most of the listening to the others' conversation
   b) contribute to the conversation equally with the others
   c) usually make all the running in the conversation

3 When communicating with someone on a one-to-one basis, which method do you feel most comfortable with?

   a) letter
   b) telephone
   c) face to face

4 When you are on a bus or train, do you ever start up a conversation with a stranger?

a) never
b) occasionally
c) usually start up some sort of conversation

5 If you were walking down the street and someone was coming towards you who you vaguely recognised, how would you behave?

a) walk past and ignore them unless they speak to you
b) give them a glance and sort of half nod
c) speak to them and attempt to engage them in some sort of conversation to find out how you know them

6 Would you take part in a karaoki competition?

a) you must be joking
b) maybe
c) just try and stop me

7 How often do you tell jokes in the company of others?

a) never
b) sometimes
c) often

8 How often do you speak at meetings?

a) hardly ever
b) sometimes
c) very often

9 Do you ever chat up members of the opposite sex?

   a) never
   b) occasionally
   c) often

10 Would you ever take part in an amateur stage
    production?

    a) no way
    b) I might if pressed
    c) yes, I would love to

11 When meeting someone for the first time, how do you
    feel?

    a) awkward and nervous
    b) at ease and interested in getting to know them
    c) bursting to tell them all about yourself

12 At the end of a dinner party when saying goodbye to a
    guest of the opposite sex, what would you prefer to do?

    a) just shake their hand
    b) shake their hand and pat them on the arm
    c) shake their hand and kiss them on both cheeks

13 When having a one-to-one conversation with someone,
    what would you prefer to do?

    a) listen to them talking about what they have been
        doing recently
    b) talk equally about what each of you have been doing
    c) tell them mainly about what you have been doing

14 In a crowded lift, what do you do?

   a) keep yourself to yourself and hardly notice the other
      people
   b) don't say much but usually have a good look at the
      people in the lift with you
   c) usually try to make some witty remark to the other
      people in the lift

15 At the works dinner you are sitting at a table with 20
   other people. How much conversation do you make?

   a) I speak very little but listen to other people and get
      on with my meal
   b) usually I speak mainly just to the people on either
      side of me
   c) I do tend to make quite a bit of the general
      conversation round the table

16 You are walking along in the town centre and the BBC
   are conducting random interviews with people on a
   certain topic. How do you behave?

   a) turn in the other direction or cross over to the other
      side of the street to ignore them
   b) say a few words for the camera if approached
   c) go out of your way to make sure that they ask you

17 You work in an office and the company board chair walks
   through. How do you react?

   a) keep you head down and hope the chair doesn't even
      notice you
   b) carry on as normal and speak if appropriate
   c) make sure that you have some sort of conversation

18 You are attending a function at which some important and influential people will also be attending. What would you wear?

a) what I would normally wear to any other function
b) I would probably buy something new for the occasion
c) I would make sure that I was wearing something to make me stand out from the crowd

19 How often do you push for promotion at work?

a) never
b) sometimes
c) often

20 What would be your reaction if you were asked to make a speech in front of a large group of people?

a) terrified at the prospect
b) I would try to prepare and make a good job of it even though it was not something that I would choose to do
c) I would be pleased and excited at the prospect

21 How often do you sunbathe in your swim-wear in the back garden in view of the neighbours?

a) never
b) occasionally
c) often

22 You are at a club and the singer asks for volunteers to go up on stage to help out with a number. How would you behave?

a) never ever volunteer
b) might possibly volunteer
c) be up on stage in a flash

23 When you are worried about something, how do you behave?

a) bottle it up inside you
b) discuss it with close friends and family
c) discuss it with as many people as you can

24 If you are in the company of people who start telling risque jokes, how do you react?

a) I feel very embarrassed and wish they would shut up
b) I don't particularly approve but am not embarrassed
c) I match them joke for joke

25 If a rather loud verbal argument broke out between two colleagues at work, how would you respond?

a) keep your head down and leave well alone
b) perhaps try to calm things down if you thought it wise to do so in the circumstances
c) almost always get involved with relish either by joining in or trying to calm things down

Assessment

Award yourself 2 points for every 'c' answer, 1 point for every 'b' and 0 points for every 'a'.

40–50 points
You are most certainly not a shrinking violet. In fact, you are

brimming with self-confidence. While this is not a bad thing, you should be careful at all times not to be too much of an extrovert to the point that people find you excessively pushy, even overbearing. Just remember that your bubbly personality should perhaps be tempered with some degree of modesty and sensitivity towards others.

25–39 points

You are no shrinking violet, even though you sometimes may think you are, but at the same time you don't push yourself beyond what to most people is an acceptable degree of behaviour. If you feel you are a little shy, and backward at coming forward at times, it may be that it is because you secretly admire the way people who are more extrovert than you behave. But remember that it is these people who are in the minority and that by showing a little reserve at the right time you are probably regarded by other people as a much more appealing personality and someone who others enjoy having in their company.

Less than 25

You are what some people would call a shrinking violet, but that's the way many people are and it doesn't make you any worse a person than someone who is excessively outgoing. Many people are extremely modest and shy but at the same time have the ability to be high achievers in their own field, providing that they can recognise their own talents and gain that bit of extra self-confidence to harness their potential. Remember that many people who appear loud and pushy are actually inwardly shy, and lack self-confidence. Their seemingly extrovert behaviour is sometimes their way of trying to overcome their own inner doubts.

Are you imaginative?

1 Which of the following is your favourite type of book?

   a) whodunnit
   b) encyclopedia
   c) autobiography

2 At which of the following would you prefer to spend a week's holiday?

   a) a theme park such as Oasis
   b) an apartment in London
   c) a cottage by the sea

3 How often do you doodle?

   a) quite often
   b) sometimes
   c) rarely

4 Which of these is your idea of a perfect garden?

   a) one of natural beauty with lots of wild flowers, a stream running through it and a wooded area
   b) neat and orderly with lots of formal flower beds and features
   c) a place primarily for relaxation with large lawn and hedges for privacy

5 You wish to hold a celebration bash for all your friends
and family because you have won several million pounds
on the lottery. Which of the following would be most
ideal for this celebration?

  a) take them to EuroDisney for two days
  b) hire the local town hall and throw the World's
     Greatest Ever Party
  c) take over a high-class hotel and let them all spend the
     weekend living a life of total luxury

6 Do you like repairing things?

  a) yes
  b) only if I know what is wrong and I know how to carry
     out the repair successfully.
  c) no

7 If you could start your career over again and were
guaranteed success in a chosen profession, which of the
following would you like to be?

  a) brain surgeon
  b) barrister
  c) politician

8 Which of these would you prefer to cultivate as a hobby?

  a) something artistic such as pottery
  b) some form of sporting activity
  c) collecting things, such as antiques

9 Do you like messing around on computers?

  a) yes
  b) perhaps, if I had more time
  c) no

10 If you cannot get to sleep at night, which of the following is most likely to be the reason?

a) my mind is too overactive
b) I am worried about something
c) I am not tired

11 You have a really heavy workload and tight deadlines. Which of the following options would most apply to you in this situation?

a) plan ahead and decide the most efficient way of dealing with the workload
b) prioritise the workload and do the most urgent jobs first
c) get your head down and get the work completed by sheer hard graft

12 Which of these would you prefer to give your partner as a gift at Christmas?

a) a surprise gift of something you knew they had always wanted
b) something which you had gone out on a shopping trip and chosen together
c) shopping vouchers for a large department store to enable them to choose their own gift at leisure

13 If you went to an Old Time Music Hall, which of the following speciality acts would you prefer to see?

a) conjuror
b) juggler
c) acrobat

14 Which of the following dogs would you prefer as a pet?

a) a little scamp of a dog always up to mischief
b) a well-behaved, well-groomed and affectionate dog
c) a totally devoted dog who you know would defend you and your property to the last

15 Which of these sports interests you the most?

a) golf
b) soccer
c) boxing

16 If you had the opportunity to watch one of the following Hitchcock movies, which one would you choose?

a) Psycho
b) The Birds
c) Rear Window

17 Which of these words would you say most applies to yourself?

a) whimsical
b) dynamic
c) ordinary

18 Which of the following television shows would you have most liked to have written?

a) Fawlty Towers
b) Dad's Army
c) Rising Damp

19 Which of these puzzles do you enjoy solving the most in newspapers and magazines?

a) crossword puzzles

b) anagrams
c) word searches

20 Do you believe in the paranormal?

a) I would have to say that I do
b) I am open minded on the subject
c) no

21 Which of the following most accurately reflects your views on modern art?

a) it is creative and challenges the mind
b) occasionally I have seen a piece of modern art that interests me
c) to be perfectly frank and honest I don't usually like it one little bit

22 Do you ever feel frustrated that you should be doing something more interesting with your life?

a) yes, frequently
b) sometimes
c) just occasionally

23 Which of the following would be your dream home?

a) a 19th-century mansion house with lots of rooms and corridors and steeped in history
b) a spacious farmhouse on the edge of the moors with acres of land
c) a modern five-bedroomed detached house with all mod-cons in its own grounds

24 Which of the following words best describes you?

   a) curious
   b) industrious
   c) fulfilled

25 Would you describe yourself as a follower of fashion?

   a) not really, I prefer my own thing
   b) to a certain extent
   c) yes, generally

Assessment

Award yourself 2 points for every 'a' answer, 1 point for every 'b' and 0 points for every 'c'.

35–50 points

Your score indicates that you are an extremely creative and imaginative person who is not afraid of defying convention and doing your own thing. If there is a drawback to this you may feel on occasions that you have not achieved in life what you are capable of, and because of this you sometimes feel frustrated and dissatisfied.

Because you are so imaginative, and your lifestyle often flies in the face of convention, this tends on occasions to irritate other people, which sometimes has the effect of making you rein in your creative thoughts and ideas. You should not forget, however, that your inventiveness and free thinking is one of your best assets and, if it has not done so already, will enable you to realise many of your ambitions and be a great success in life.

Let your imagination run riot, and enjoy the experience, but take great care not to upset or offend too many people in the process.

16–34 points

You are in the main a conventional and respectable person who believes that there is a time and a place for everything, including letting your hair down occasionally. You do, however, have an open mind on many things which are considered unconventional, and it may be a good idea from time to time to use your imagination and explore some of these new avenues.

Each one of us is capable of using our imagination more and your score indicates that you have the potential to be an imaginative person, if only you can, from time to time, forget convention and be a little bolder in making your aspirations come to fruition.

Below 16

While your score indicates that you are not particularly an imaginative person, this does not mean that you are unhappy with your lot in life. In fact, because you are probably a hard working and down-to-earth achiever it may be that you are more content with your lot in life than someone who is over-imaginative, and frustrated that they have not turned many of their ideas into reality.

Just occasionally, however, you may like to set aside some time to collect your own thoughts. Each one of us only uses a small fraction of our brain. We all have the potential to think more creatively and we all have an imagination, it is just that some use it more than others. Who knows, if you give yourself more thinking time, innovative ideas may suddenly start to flow. What you do with these ideas is, of course, up to you, but without new inventive ideas, none of us is ever capable of achieving anything original or exciting.

Are you honourable?

Tick the appropriate column.

		Yes	Don't know	No
1	If you found a wallet, would you hand it in to the police station?	❏	❏	❏
2	If you received a cheque in the post which wasn't for you, would you return it?	❏	❏	❏
3	Have you ever cheated on your tax return?	❏	❏	❏
4	If you saw a pick-pocket at work would you report him or her?	❏	❏	❏
5	If a shopkeeper gave you too much change, would you inform him or her?	❏	❏	❏
6	Have you ever taken a day off work and then reported sick?	❏	❏	❏
7	Would you ever tell untruths to assist your company?	❏	❏	❏
8	Do you tell white lies?	❏	❏	❏

		Yes	Don't know	No
9	If you broke a window, would you own up?	❏	❏	❏
10	Do you give the impression that you are richer than you are?	❏	❏	❏
11	Would you support your friend if he or she was telling lies?	❏	❏	❏
12	Have you ever stolen anything?	❏	❏	❏
13	Would you let a friend get punished for something that you have done?	❏	❏	❏
14	If you damaged a car in a car park, would you own up?	❏	❏	❏
15	Do you ignore signs, such as Keep Off the Grass?	❏	❏	❏

Scoring instructions

	Yes	Don't know	No
1	2	1	0
2	2	1	0
3	0	1	2
4	2	1	0
5	2	1	0
6	0	1	2
7	0	1	2
8	0	1	2
9	2	1	0
10	0	1	2
11	2	1	0
12	0	1	2
13	0	1	2
14	2	1	0
15	0	1	2

Scoring analysis

26–30	Exceedingly honest
22–25	Very honest
18–21	Above average
13–17	Average
9–12	Slightly dishonest
5–8	Dishonest
0–4	Very dishonest

Are you sensual?

Tick the appropriate column.

	Yes	Don't know	No
1 Do you keep a slim figure?	❏	❏	❏
2 Have you a perfume preference?	❏	❏	❏
3 Do you have a favourite drink?	❏	❏	❏
4 Do you enjoy walking in snow?	❏	❏	❏
5 Do smells excite you?	❏	❏	❏
6 Do you cry very easily?	❏	❏	❏
7 Do you like silk next to your skin?	❏	❏	❏
8 Are you nostalgic?	❏	❏	❏
9 Do you enjoy sunbathing?	❏	❏	❏
10 Do you enjoy new recipes?	❏	❏	❏
11 Do loud noises offend you?	❏	❏	❏
12 Do you go to massage parlours?	❏	❏	❏
13 Do you like touching people?	❏	❏	❏
14 Do you like reading risqué novels?	❏	❏	❏
15 Do you enjoy beautiful scenery?	❏	❏	❏

Scoring instructions

	Yes	Don't know	No
1	2	1	0
2	2	1	0
3	2	1	0
4	2	1	0
5	2	1	0
6	2	1	0
7	2	1	0
8	2	1	0
9	2	1	0
10	2	1	0
11	2	1	0
12	2	1	0
13	2	1	0
14	2	1	0
15	2	1	0

Scoring analysis

26–30	Exceedingly sensual
22–25	Very sensual
18–21	Above average
13–17	Average
9–12	Slightly sensual
5–8	Not very sensual
0–4	Lacking in sensuality

Are you thrifty?

Tick the appropriate column.

		Yes	Don't know	No
1	Do you pay bills immediately you receive them?	❏	❏	❏
2	Do you walk to save fares?	❏	❏	❏
3	Do you know your bank balance at any time?	❏	❏	❏
4	Do you always buy a bargain when you see it?	❏	❏	❏
5	Do you find the cheapest goods to buy?	❏	❏	❏
6	Do you squeeze every last drop out of a toothpaste tube?	❏	❏	❏
7	Do you haggle to bring prices down so that you can afford to buy?	❏	❏	❏
8	Do you switch off lights when leaving a room?	❏	❏	❏

	Yes	Don't know	No
9 Do you owe money on your credit card?	❏	❏	❏
10 Are you an impulsive buyer?	❏	❏	❏
11 Do you buy cheaper brands of food than the best brands?	❏	❏	❏
12 Do you buy a newspaper every day?	❏	❏	❏
13 Do you give regularly to charities?	❏	❏	❏
14 If you won some money, would you spend it quickly?	❏	❏	❏
15 Do you save a weekly amount and leave it there?	❏	❏	❏

Scoring instructions

	Yes	Don't know	No
1	2	1	0
2	2	1	0
3	2	1	0
4	2	1	0
5	2	1	0
6	2	1	0
7	2	1	0
8	2	1	0
9	0	1	2
10	0	1	2
11	2	1	0
12	0	1	2
13	0	1	2
14	0	1	2
15	2	1	0

Scoring analysis

26–30	Exceedingly thrifty
22–25	Very thrifty
18–21	Slightly thrifty
13–17	Average
9–12	Spends too much
5–8	Careless with money
0–4	A spendthrift

Have you good humour?

Tick the appropriate column.

	Yes	Don't know	No
1 Do you go to pantomimes?	❏	❏	❏
2 Do you get embarrassed if you fall over?	❏	❏	❏
3 Have you a joke book in your house?	❏	❏	❏
4 Do you find most humour is childish?	❏	❏	❏
5 Do you get annoyed if people laugh at you?	❏	❏	❏
6 Have you ever laughed in church?	❏	❏	❏
7 Do you make practical jokes?	❏	❏	❏
8 Would you rather see an amusing film instead of a drama?	❏	❏	❏
9 Do you laugh at least once a day?	❏	❏	❏

	Yes	Don't know	No
10 Do you like comedy shows on television?	❑	❑	❑
11 Would you laugh if someone slipped on a banana skin?	❑	❑	❑
12 Do you like risqué jokes?	❑	❑	❑
13 Do you ever laugh at yourself?	❑	❑	❑
14 Do you sometimes laugh when you are alone?	❑	❑	❑
15 Do you get annoyed if somebody laughs at a colleague?	❑	❑	❑

Scoring instructions

	Yes	Don't know	No
1	2	1	0
2	0	1	2
3	2	1	0
4	0	1	2
5	0	1	2
6	2	1	0
7	2	1	0
8	2	1	0
9	2	1	0
10	2	1	0
11	2	1	0
12	2	1	0
13	2	1	0
14	2	1	0
15	0	1	2

Scoring analysis

26–30	Excellent humour
22–25	Good humour
18–21	Above average
13–17	Average
9–12	Below average
5–8	Slight humour
0–4	No humour

Are you daring?

Tick the appropriate column.

	Yes	Don't know	No
1 Would you go on a mountaineering trip?	❏	❏	❏
2 Do you dive at the swimming pool?	❏	❏	❏
3 Would you like to open a shop?	❏	❏	❏
4 Do you dislike fast rides at the fairground?	❏	❏	❏
5 Do you drink intoxicating liquor more than you should?	❏	❏	❏
6 Would you interfere if two men were fighting?	❏	❏	❏
7 Would you go deep sea diving?	❏	❏	❏
8 Do you insure your household appliances against failure?	❏	❏	❏
9 Do you smoke?	❏	❏	❏

	Yes	Don't know	No
10 Would you walk through a cemetery at night?	❏	❏	❏
11 Would you tackle a burglar?	❏	❏	❏
12 Do you regularly drive above the speed limit?	❏	❏	❏
13 Do you like horror films?	❏	❏	❏
14 Have you ever smuggled goods through customs?	❏	❏	❏
15 Would you change into your bathing costume on the beach?	❏	❏	❏

Scoring instructions

	Yes	Don't know	No
1	2	1	0
2	2	1	0
3	2	1	0
4	0	1	2
5	2	1	0
6	2	1	0
7	2	1	0
8	0	1	2
9	2	1	0
10	2	1	0
11	2	1	0
12	2	1	0
13	2	1	0
14	2	1	0
15	2	1	0

Scoring analysis

26–30	Very daring
22–25	Daring
18–21	Slightly daring
13–17	Average
9–12	Slightly timid
5–8	Timid
0–4	Very timid

Domination

Tick the appropriate column.

	Yes	Don't know	No
1 Do you get annoyed easily?	❏	❏	❏
2 Do you speak your mind even if it upsets some people?	❏	❏	❏
3 Do you like making other people embarrassed?	❏	❏	❏
4 Do you think that you could make a better show on television than you see?	❏	❏	❏
5 Do you ever take over at social functions?	❏	❏	❏
6 Do you dislike conventional rules?	❏	❏	❏
7 Are you intolerant of other people's ideas?	❏	❏	❏
8 Do you always like to get your own way?	❏	❏	❏

	Yes	Don't know	No
9 Do you use bad language in an argument?	❏	❏	❏
10 Do you invest in shares for a quick profit?	❏	❏	❏
11 Do you ignore signs such as 'Beware of the Bull'?	❏	❏	❏
12 Do you start road rage incidents?	❏	❏	❏
13 Do you get annoyed at opinions that you disagree with?	❏	❏	❏
14 Do you think that your own sex is cleverer than the opposite sex?	❏	❏	❏
15 Do you think that you are more intelligent than most people?	❏	❏	❏

Scoring instructions

	Yes	Don't know	No
1	2	1	0
2	2	1	0
3	2	1	0
4	2	1	0
5	2	1	0
6	2	1	0
7	2	1	0
8	2	1	0
9	2	1	0
10	2	1	0
11	2	1	0
12	2	1	0
13	2	1	0
14	2	1	0
15	2	1	0

Scoring analysis

26–30	Exceedingly dominant
22–25	Very dominant
18–21	Slightly dominant
13–17	Average
9–12	Carefree
5–8	Easy going
0–4	Placid

Are you a worrier?

Tick the appropriate column.

	Yes	Don't know	No
1 Are you nervous at a job interview?	❏	❏	❏
2 Do you worry about your finances?	❏	❏	❏
3 Are you a nervous driver?	❏	❏	❏
4 Do you worry about getting fat?	❏	❏	❏
5 Do you sleep badly?	❏	❏	❏
6 Do you like taking on responsibilities?	❏	❏	❏
7 Are you self-conscious?	❏	❏	❏
8 Would you be unhappy going solo on the stage?	❏	❏	❏
9 Do you worry over trivialities?	❏	❏	❏
10 Do you visit your doctor frequently?	❏	❏	❏
11 Do you worry if you are going bald?	❏	❏	❏

	Yes	Don't know	No
12 Do you get upset if people make fun of you?	❏	❏	❏
13 Do you get worried when you have to meet new people?	❏	❏	❏
14 Do you pay your bills immediately you receive them?	❏	❏	❏
15 Do you get startled by sudden noises?	❏	❏	❏

Scoring instructions

	Yes	Don't know	No
1	2	1	0
2	2	1	0
3	2	1	0
4	2	1	0
5	2	1	0
6	0	1	2
7	2	1	0
8	2	1	0
9	2	1	0
10	2	1	0
11	2	1	0
12	2	1	0
13	2	1	0
14	2	1	0
15	2	1	0

Scoring analysis

26–30	Very worried
22–25	Worried
18–21	Slightly worried
13–17	Average
9–12	Occasionally worried
5–8	Unworried
0–4	Not the least worried

Are you absent minded?

Tick the appropriate column.

	Yes	Don't know	No
1 Do you ever get names mixed up?	❑	❑	❑
2 Have you ever lost your wallet?	❑	❑	❑
3 If you have no watch on, can you judge the time?	❑	❑	❑
4 Have you ever gone past your stop on a bus or train?	❑	❑	❑
5 Do you always remember your car number?	❑	❑	❑
6 Can you always remember phone numbers?	❑	❑	❑
7 Do you often walk home from the shops, and forget you went by car?	❑	❑	❑
8 Do you remember everybody's birthday?	❑	❑	❑

	Yes	Don't know	No
9 Do you ever go into a room and forget what you came in for?	❏	❏	❏
10 Have you ever got lost while driving a car?	❏	❏	❏
11 Do you ever wear odd socks?	❏	❏	❏
12 Have you ever left an umbrella in a restaurant?	❏	❏	❏
13 Have you ever forgotten an appointment?	❏	❏	❏
14 Do you tend to day dream?	❏	❏	❏
15 Can you remember poetry?	❏	❏	❏

Scoring instructions

	Yes	Don't know	No
1	2	1	0
2	2	1	0
3	0	1	2
4	2	1	0
5	2	1	0
6	2	1	0
7	2	1	0
8	2	1	0
9	2	1	0
10	2	1	0
11	2	1	0
12	2	1	0
13	2	1	0
14	2	1	0
15	0	1	2

Scoring analysis

26–30	Exceedingly absent minded
22–25	Very absent minded
18–21	Slightly absent minded
13–17	Normal
9–12	Nearly normal
5–8	Slightly absent minded
0–4	Not the least absent minded

Do you like work?

Tick the appropriate column.

	Yes	Don't know	No
1 Do you get restless if you are doing nothing?	❏	❏	❏
2 Do you play much sport?	❏	❏	❏
3 Do you find it difficult to relax?	❏	❏	❏
4 Do you rise early?	❏	❏	❏
5 Do you regularly spend Sunday morning in bed?	❏	❏	❏
6 Do you work while eating lunch?	❏	❏	❏
7 Have you ever worked instead of going on holiday?	❏	❏	❏
8 Do you have a second job?	❏	❏	❏
9 Do you wake up and worry about work?	❏	❏	❏

	Yes	Don't know	No
10 Does your family complain that you work long hours?	❏	❏	❏
11 Do you often work overtime?	❏	❏	❏
12 Do you want promotion at work?	❏	❏	❏
13 Would you cover for a sick colleague at work?	❏	❏	❏
14 Do you enjoy your work?	❏	❏	❏
15 If it was necessary to work unpaid would you work?	❏	❏	❏

Scoring instructions

	Yes	Don't know	No
1	2	1	0
2	2	1	0
3	2	1	0
4	2	1	0
5	0	1	2
6	2	1	0
7	2	1	0
8	2	1	0
9	2	1	0
10	2	1	0
11	2	1	0
12	2	1	0
13	2	1	0
14	2	1	0
15	2	1	0

Scoring analysis

26–30	You are a workaholic
22–25	Hard worker
18–21	Above average
13–17	Average
9–12	Below average
5–8	You are lazy
0–4	You are exceedingly lazy

Are you sociable?

Tick the appropriate column.

	Yes	Don't know	No
1 Do you talk to people in the supermarket?	❏	❏	❏
2 Do you make many new acquaintances?	❏	❏	❏
3 Do you make friends easily?	❏	❏	❏
4 Do you enjoy friends staying for a weekend at your house?	❏	❏	❏
5 Do you do voluntary work in your town or village?	❏	❏	❏
6 Do you often play table games?	❏	❏	❏
7 Do you like noisy holiday resorts?	❏	❏	❏
8 Would you like to organise an office party?	❏	❏	❏
9 Do you get on well with children?	❏	❏	❏

	Yes	Don't know	No
10 Do you like pets?	❏	❏	❏
11 Are you the life and soul of a party?	❏	❏	❏
12 Do you always make friends on every holiday?	❏	❏	❏
13 Do you reply to letters immediately?	❏	❏	❏
14 Do you go to the theatre often?	❏	❏	❏
15 Do you help an old person living locally?	❏	❏	❏

Scoring instructions

	Yes	Don't know	No
1	2	1	0
2	2	1	0
3	2	1	0
4	2	1	0
5	2	1	0
6	2	1	0
7	2	1	0
8	2	1	0
9	2	1	0
10	2	1	0
11	2	1	0
12	2	1	0
13	2	1	0
14	2	1	0
15	2	1	0

Scoring analysis

26–30	Exceedingly sociable
22–25	Very sociable
18–21	Sociable
13–17	Pleasant
9–12	Unsociable
5–8	Very unsociable
0–4	Exceedingly unsociable

Are you emotional?

Tick the appropriate column.

	Yes	Don't know	No
1 Do you get excited at football matches?	❏	❏	❏
2 Do you kiss people you like?	❏	❏	❏
3 Do you talk to strangers in the supermarket?	❏	❏	❏
4 Do you envy success in others?	❏	❏	❏
5 Do you lose your temper easily?	❏	❏	❏
6 Do you keep a dog or cat?	❏	❏	❏
7 Do you enjoy pantomimes?	❏	❏	❏
8 Have you ever had an argument with a neighbour?	❏	❏	❏
9 Do you tell risqué jokes?	❏	❏	❏
10 Do you enjoy the company of children?	❏	❏	❏

	Yes	Don't know	No
11 Do you dislike politicians?	❏	❏	❏
12 As an adult have you ever cried?	❏	❏	❏
13 Have you been involved in a road rage incident?	❏	❏	❏
14 Are there some people whom you dislike intensely?	❏	❏	❏
15 Are you easily embarrassed?	❏	❏	❏

Scoring instructions

	Yes	Don't know	No
1	2	1	0
2	2	1	0
3	2	1	0
4	0	1	2
5	2	1	0
6	2	1	0
7	2	1	0
8	2	1	0
9	2	1	0
10	2	1	0
11	2	1	0
12	2	1	0
13	2	1	0
14	2	1	0
15	2	1	0

Scoring analysis

26–30	Exceedingly emotional
22–25	Very emotional
18–21	Slightly emotional
13–17	Balanced
9–12	Slightly unemotional
5–8	Very unemotional
0–4	Exceedingly unemotional

Extroversion

Tick the appropriate column.

		Yes	Don't know	No
1	Have you ever been injured playing dangerous sports?	❏	❏	❏
2	Would you like to direct a play on the stage?	❏	❏	❏
3	Would you like to be a pilot?	❏	❏	❏
4	If you had a prison sentence, would you study for a degree?	❏	❏	❏
5	Have you ever complained in a shop to a manager or assistant?	❏	❏	❏
6	Would you like to take part in a road rally?	❏	❏	❏
7	Would you be in charge of a float in a pageant?	❏	❏	❏
8	Have you many friends?	❏	❏	❏

	Yes	Don't know	No
9 Do you like going to night class?	❏	❏	❏
10 Are you popular at your work?	❏	❏	❏
11 Would you like to work in finance in a big city?	❏	❏	❏
12 Would you like to be a politician?	❏	❏	❏
13 Are you a good public speaker?	❏	❏	❏
14 Would you like to be a doctor?	❏	❏	❏
15 Are you an energetic person?	❏	❏	❏

Scoring instructions

	Yes	Don't know	No
1	2	1	0
2	2	1	0
3	2	1	0
4	2	1	0
5	2	1	0
6	2	1	0
7	2	1	0
8	2	1	0
9	2	1	0
10	2	1	0
11	2	1	0
12	2	1	0
13	2	1	0
14	2	1	0
15	2	1	0

Scoring analysis

26–30	Extremely extroverted
22–25	Very extroverted
18–21	Slightly extroverted
13–17	Balanced
9–12	Slightly introverted
5–8	Very introverted
0–4	Extremely introverted

Aggression

Tick the appropriate column.

		Yes	Don't know	No
1	Would you report a pick-pocket if you saw one?	❏	❏	❏
2	Do you believe that policemen should be armed?	❏	❏	❏
3	Do you always ride on the big dipper at fun-fairs?	❏	❏	❏
4	Would you ride in a submarine?	❏	❏	❏
5	Would you like to be an all-in wrestler?	❏	❏	❏
6	Would you go on a safari?	❏	❏	❏
7	Do you prefer action films to love stories?	❏	❏	❏
8	Have you ever been in a fight?	❏	❏	❏
9	Would you like a position in MI5?	❏	❏	❏

	Yes	Don't know	No
10 Would you pick up a live rat?	❏	❏	❏
11 Would you attack an intruder on your property?	❏	❏	❏
12 Do you like debates?	❏	❏	❏
13 Would you do a bunjee jump?	❏	❏	❏
14 Would you argue with the other driver in a road incident?	❏	❏	❏
15 Do you like horror films?	❏	❏	❏

Scoring instructions

	Yes	Don't know	No
1	2	1	0
2	2	1	0
3	2	1	0
4	2	1	0
5	2	1	0
6	2	1	0
7	2	1	0
8	2	1	0
9	2	1	0
10	2	1	0
11	2	1	0
12	2	1	0
13	2	1	0
14	2	1	0
15	2	1	0

Scoring analysis

26–30	Exceedingly aggressive
22–25	Fiery
18–21	Slightly aggressive
13–17	Balanced
9–12	Not very aggressive
5–8	Slightly timid
0–4	Timid

Are you artistic?

Tick the appropriate column.

	Yes	Don't know	No
1 Do you read glossy magazines for interior design, for ideas for your house?	❏	❏	❏
2 Do you travel to areas for the scenic views?	❏	❏	❏
3 Are your clothes fashionable?	❏	❏	❏
4 Have you ever joined a flower arranging class?	❏	❏	❏
5 Do you have a library ticket?	❏	❏	❏
6 Are you a watercolour painter?	❏	❏	❏
7 Have you ever written a short story?	❏	❏	❏
8 Do you visit stately homes?	❏	❏	❏
9 Do you often frequent art galleries?	❏	❏	❏

	Yes	Don't know	No
10 Do you like poetry?	❏	❏	❏
11 Are you a keen gardener?	❏	❏	❏
12 Are you a keen photographer?	❏	❏	❏
13 Are you good at DIY?	❏	❏	❏
14 Would you like to be an architect?	❏	❏	❏
15 Would you like to be an illustrator for a comic publication?	❏	❏	❏

Scoring instructions

	Yes	Don't know	No
1	2	1	0
2	2	1	0
3	2	1	0
4	2	1	0
5	2	1	0
6	2	1	0
7	2	1	0
8	2	1	0
9	2	1	0
10	2	1	0
11	2	1	0
12	2	1	0
13	2	1	0
14	2	1	0
15	2	1	0

Scoring analysis

26–30	Exceedingly artistic
22–25	Very artistic
18–21	Slightly artistic
13–17	Average
9–12	Just below average
5–8	Not very artistic
0–4	Not artistic

Ambition

Tick the appropriate column.

	Yes	Don't know	No
1 Do you tend to spend more than you can afford?	❏	❏	❏
2 Do you wear clothes that are in the latest fashion?	❏	❏	❏
3 Have you many rich acquaintances?	❏	❏	❏
4 Do you like taking tests or exams?	❏	❏	❏
5 Would you tell a lie if it improved your chances of promotion?	❏	❏	❏
6 Would you like to work in television?	❏	❏	❏
7 Are you a good public speaker?	❏	❏	❏
8 Would you work abroad if you were promoted?	❏	❏	❏
9 Would you like to be a film star?	❏	❏	❏

	Yes	Don't know	No
10 Would you study hard for a degree?	❏	❏	❏
11 Do you dislike losing at games?	❏	❏	❏
12 Would you like a bigger and newer car than the one you have?	❏	❏	❏
13 Do you belong to a chess club?	❏	❏	❏
14 Would you stand for a post in local government?	❏	❏	❏
15 Would you like to run your own business?	❏	❏	❏

Scoring instructions

	Yes	Don't know	No
1	2	1	0
2	2	1	0
3	2	1	0
4	2	1	0
5	2	1	0
6	2	1	0
7	2	1	0
8	2	1	0
9	2	1	0
10	2	1	0
11	2	1	0
12	2	1	0
13	2	1	0
14	2	1	0
15	2	1	0

Scoring analysis

26–30	Exceedingly ambitious
22–25	Very ambitious
18–21	Slightly ambitious
13–17	Average
9–12	Slightly ambitious
5–8	Not very ambitious
0–4	Exceedingly unambitious

Are you tolerant?

Tick the appropriate column.

	Yes	Don't know	No
1 Do you think that your nationality is better than any other?	❏	❏	❏
2 Do you object to noisy children?	❏	❏	❏
3 Would you object if your daughter was involved with a person of dubious character?	❏	❏	❏
4 Do you believe that tolerant teachers are responsible for bad behaviour?	❏	❏	❏
5 Do you have many friends who are divorcees?	❏	❏	❏
6 Do you think that lower moral standards are increasing?	❏	❏	❏
7 Do you dislike people who are not married but living together?	❏	❏	❏

	Yes	Don't know	No
8 Do you object to religious sects knocking on your door?	❏	❏	❏
9 Do you think punishment for offenders should be increased?	❏	❏	❏
10 Do you object to cats in your garden?	❏	❏	❏
11 Do you think that women should take up posts in the churches?	❏	❏	❏
12 Do you frequent noisy parties?	❏	❏	❏
13 Do you object to mobile phones on trains?	❏	❏	❏
14 Would you object if a home for juvenile deliquents opened in your road?	❏	❏	❏
15 Have you noisy neighbours who do not associate with you?	❏	❏	❏

Scoring instructions

	Yes	Don't know	No
1	0	1	2
2	0	1	2
3	0	1	2
4	0	1	2
5	2	1	0
6	0	1	2
7	0	1	2
8	0	1	2
9	0	1	2
10	0	1	2
11	2	1	0
12	2	1	0
13	0	1	2
14	0	1	2
15	0	1	2

Scoring analysis

26–30	Exceedingly tolerant
22–25	Tolerant
18–21	Slightly tolerant
13–17	Average
9–12	Slightly intolerant
5–8	Intolerant
0–4	Exceedingly intolerant

Imagination

Tick the appropriate column.

	Yes	Don't know	No
1 Could you write poetry?	❏	❏	❏
2 Do you believe that there are aliens somewhere in the universe?	❏	❏	❏
3 Do you believe in the supernatural?	❏	❏	❏
4 Could you write a children's book?	❏	❏	❏
5 Would you stay in a haunted house alone at night time?	❏	❏	❏
6 Do you believe in life after death?	❏	❏	❏
7 Do you believe in poltergeists?	❏	❏	❏
8 Do you dream most nights?	❏	❏	❏
9 Do you believe in spiritualism?	❏	❏	❏

	Yes	Don't know	No
10 Do you ever plan what you would do if you won the Lottery?	❏	❏	❏
11 Do you believe that there is a Loch Ness monster?	❏	❏	❏
12 Do you get frightened when you go out in the dark?	❏	❏	❏
13 Would you have liked to live in the 19th century?	❏	❏	❏
14 Would you like to go to the moon?	❏	❏	❏
15 Do you daydream?	❏	❏	❏

Scoring instructions

	Yes	Don't know	No
1	2	1	0
2	2	1	0
3	2	1	0
4	2	1	0
5	2	1	0
6	2	1	0
7	2	1	0
8	2	1	0
9	2	1	0
10	2	1	0
11	2	1	0
12	2	1	0
13	2	1	0
14	2	1	0
15	2	1	0

Scoring analysis

26–30	Strong imagination
22–25	Good imagination
18–21	Slightly imaginative
13–17	Average
9–12	Below average
5–8	Little imagination
0–4	Very unimaginative

Are you obsessive?

Tick the appropriate column.

	Yes	Don't know	No
1 Do untidy people annoy you?	❑	❑	❑
2 Do you worry about jobs left undone?	❑	❑	❑
3 Do you wash your hands more than four times a day?	❑	❑	❑
4 Is it true to say that you never walk under a ladder?	❑	❑	❑
5 Do you keep all of your papers in strict order?	❑	❑	❑
6 Do you always know how much money you have in your wallet?	❑	❑	❑
7 Are you good at packing for a holiday?	❑	❑	❑
8 Do you wash the crockery immediately after a meal?	❑	❑	❑

	Yes	Don't know	No
9 Do you start buying next year's Christmas cards immediately after Christmas?	❏	❏	❏
10 Do you keep up to date with your letter writing?	❏	❏	❏
11 Are you never late for appointments?	❏	❏	❏
12 Do you always make sure all the doors are locked at night?	❏	❏	❏
13 Are your shoes always well polished?	❏	❏	❏
14 Have you never lost a key?	❏	❏	❏
15 Do you clear up immediately after a party?	❏	❏	❏

Scoring instructions

	Yes	Don't know	No
1	2	1	0
2	2	1	0
3	2	1	0
4	2	1	0
5	2	1	0
6	2	1	0
7	2	1	0
8	2	1	0
9	2	1	0
10	2	1	0
11	2	1	0
12	2	1	0
13	2	1	0
14	2	1	0
15	2	1	0

Scoring analysis

26–30	Exceedingly obsessive
22–25	Very obsessive
18–21	Slightly above average
13–17	Average
9–12	Slightly obsessive
5–8	Not very obsessive
0–4	Not obsessive

Are you assertive?

Tick the appropriate column.

	Yes	Don't know	No
1 If your meal in a restaurant was not to your liking, would you complain?	❏	❏	❏
2 Are you afraid of persons in authority?	❏	❏	❏
3 Would you refuse a suggestion that you should stand for chair of a club?	❏	❏	❏
4 If the telephone rang just as you were going out, would you tell the caller to ring later?	❏	❏	❏
5 Would you complain if your wine had a small piece of cork in it?	❏	❏	❏
6 If a neighbour asked to borrow your mower, would you refuse?	❏	❏	❏
7 If an appliance went wrong, would you complain to head office, even if it was repaired?	❏	❏	❏

	Yes	Don't know	No
8 You are trying to diet and you are given a box of chocolates. Would you eat them?	❏	❏	❏
9 If you are kept waiting at the doctor's surgery, would you complain?	❏	❏	❏
10 A local cat digs up your garden flowers. Would you complain?	❏	❏	❏
11 If the dog next door kept on barking, would you object?	❏	❏	❏
12 If you are not happy about your car repairs would you complain to the garage?	❏	❏	❏
13 Would you object to a passenger smoking on a non-smoking train?	❏	❏	❏
14 Do you find it difficult to take advice from other people?	❏	❏	❏
15 If a salesperson was not attentive to your request, would you complain?	❏	❏	❏

Scoring instructions

	Yes	Don't know	No
1	2	1	0
2	0	1	2
3	2	1	0
4	2	1	0
5	2	1	0
6	2	1	0
7	2	1	0
8	0	1	2
9	2	1	0
10	2	1	0
11	2	1	0
12	2	1	0
13	2	1	0
14	2	1	0
15	2	1	0

Scoring analysis

26–30	Exceedingly assertive
22–25	Assertive
18–21	Slightly assertive
13–17	Mild
9–12	Very mild
5–8	Placid
0–4	Very placid

Are you optimistic?

Tick the appropriate column.

	Yes	Don't know	No
1 Would you lend money to a friend?	❏	❏	❏
2 Do you expect to be promoted at work in the next five years?	❏	❏	❏
3 Do you possess a burglar alarm?	❏	❏	❏
4 Do you regularly have wagers on horses?	❏	❏	❏
5 Do you have a very good pension scheme which you have taken out privately?	❏	❏	❏
6 Do you trust acquaintances?	❏	❏	❏
7 If you had to see a specialist would you expect bad news?	❏	❏	❏
8 Do you hide valuables in your home when you are away on holiday?	❏	❏	❏

	Yes	Don't know	No
9 Do you have a large insurance policy on your life?	❏	❏	❏
10 Do you always take an umbrella if the weather is doubtful?	❏	❏	❏
11 Do you regularly purchase Lottery tickets?	❏	❏	❏
12 Are you a spendthrift?	❏	❏	❏
13 Do you anticipate the train being late?	❏	❏	❏
14 Do you dream frequently?	❏	❏	❏
15 Are you an early riser?	❏	❏	❏

Scoring instructions

	Yes	Don't know	No
1	2	1	0
2	2	1	0
3	0	1	2
4	2	1	0
5	0	1	2
6	2	1	0
7	0	1	2
8	0	1	2
9	0	1	2
10	0	1	2
11	2	1	0
12	2	1	0
13	0	1	2
14	2	1	0
15	2	1	0

Scoring analysis

26–30	Very optimistic
22–25	Optimistic
18–21	Slightly optimistic
13–17	Careful
9–12	Slightly pessimistic
5–8	Pessimistic
0–4	Very pessimistic

Section 2
Aptitude tests

Aptitude tests

This section consists of two separate IQ tests each of 40 questions. Within each of these tests are four sub-tests, each of 10 questions, in four different disciplines: spatial ability, logical thought processes, verbal ability and numerical ability in Test One, and verbal ability, numerical ability, maths and diagrams in Test Two. It is these disciplines that are most common in aptitude testing.

Because these tests have been specially compiled for this book and have not, therefore been standardised, an actual IQ rating cannot be given. We do, however, give a performance rating for each test of 10 questions to enable you to identify your own strengths or weaknesses, and we also give an overall rating for each complete test of 40 questions. It is this overall rating which is the best guide to your performance.

You should keep strictly within the time limit otherwise your score will be invalidated.

10-question test (time limit 30 minutes):
10 exceptional 8–9 excellent 7 very good
 5–6 good   4 average

40-question test (time limit 2 hours):
36–40 exceptional 31–35 excellent 25–30 very good
19–24 good   14–18 average

IQ test one

Spatial ability test

Read the instruction to each question and study each set of diagrams carefully.

1 Sequence

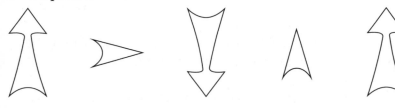

What comes next in the above sequence?

A	B	C	D

2 Similarity

Which box below has most in common with the box above?

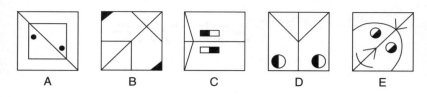

A   B   C   D   E

3   Cube

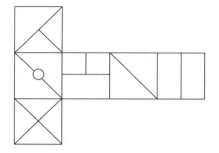

When the above is folded to form a cube, which is the only one of the following that can be produced?

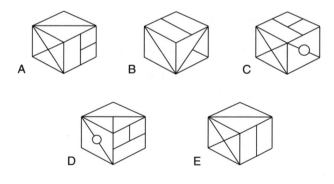

A   B   C

D   E

4   Which is the odd one out?

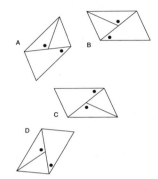

5   Squares

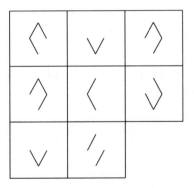

Which is the missing square?

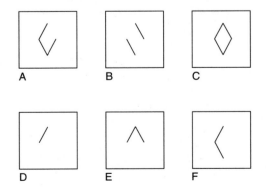

6   Missing piece

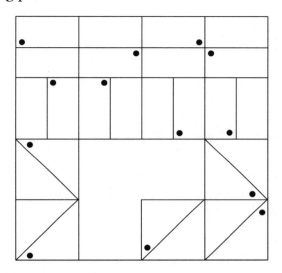

Which is the missing piece?

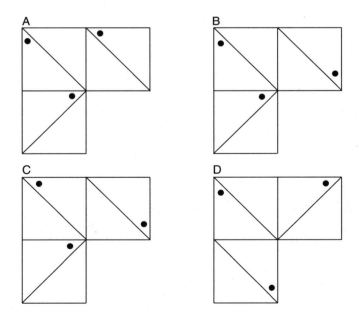

7   Sequence

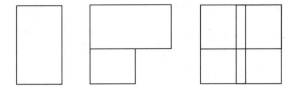

What comes next in the above sequence?

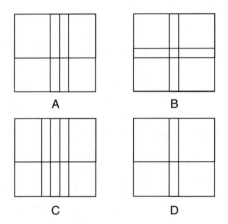

8   Sequence

What comes next in the above sequence?

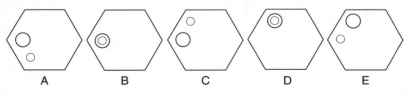

9 Comparison

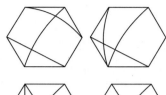

 is to:

as   is to:

| A | B | C | D | E |

10 Sequence

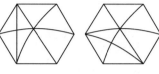

What comes next?

A   B   C   D

Logic test

1   Which word continues this sequence?

ABDICATES, ESTABLISH, HISTORICAL, CLARIFIED

Is it: deafening, edition, calamity or idolise?

2   Five men take part in a race. Jack finished either second, third or fourth. Alan was not the winner. Sam finished one place behind Alan. John did not finish in second place. Gerald was two places behind John. Who finished in second place?

3   Which number is the odd one out?

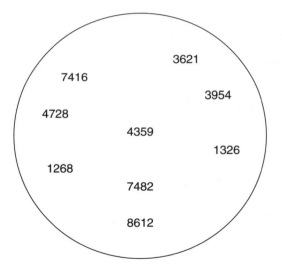

4   What number should replace the question mark?

121, 2112, 2122, 1132, ?

5   What word is missing?

     remit, elude, muser, ? , terse

6   34821 is to 12743

and   75968 is to 86857

as   39284 is to   ?

7   What number should replace the question mark?

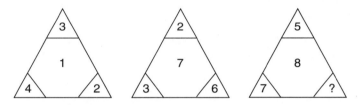

8   NEW is to LIT as TAG is to   ?

9   What comes next?

     A   AB   ABD   ABDG   ?

10   EXTRA, DEAREST, RAYON, ESTABLISH

     Which of the following words would you logically choose
     to add to the above list?

     apply, invoke, feel, copious

Verbal ability test

1   Which word in brackets is similar in meaning to the word in capitals?

NEFARIOUS (lax, petty, atrocious, manic, incessant)

2   KEPT OWN TEA is an anagram of which two words that are opposite in meaning?

3   Which two of the following words are most nearly opposite in meaning?

CULPABLE, REPRESSIVE, REPUGNANT, EVOCATIVE, DEMOCRATIC, PACIFIC

4   SHOCK is to OUTBURST as TRAUMA is to: hysteria, obsession, neurosis, paroxysm, catharsis

5   What is the meaning of sinistral?

a) S-shaped
b) curving gracefully
c) hollowed out
d) left-handed
e) corrupt

6   Choose four words that if swapped round would make this sentence comprehensible:

Today, some of the longer cases of academia are found in verbosity where arguments are judged to be more impressive the worst it takes to express them.

7 Which word is the odd one out?

CLINCH, DEBUT, ULTIMATUM, FAREWELL, EPILOGUE,
CULMINATE

8 Change one letter only in each word to produce a
familiar phrase:

HE IS ACE ON

9 Which two of the following words are most alike in
meaning?

QUESTIONABLE, QUERULOUS, PRETENTIOUS,
PETULANT, VIABLE

10 JOIE DE VIVRE is to HIGH SPIRITS as QUID PRO QUO is
to:
a) open to question
b) quick witted
c) on top of the world
d) tit for tat
e) at the double

Numerical ability test

1 How many minutes before 1 p.m. is it, if 88 minutes ago it was three times as many minutes past 10 a.m.?

2 What number should replace the question mark?

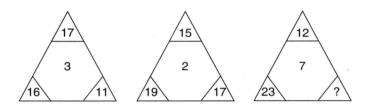

3 What comes next?

13, 17, 29, 52, 82, ?

4 What number should replace the question mark?

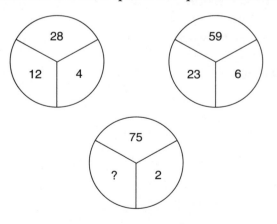

5   Which two numbers should replace the question marks?

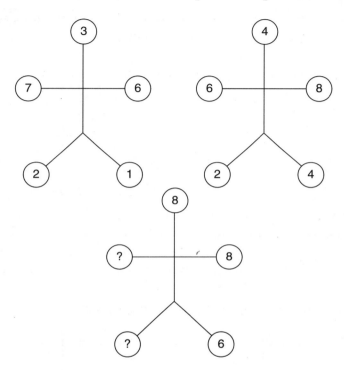

6   Scores

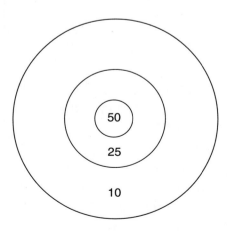

On which target has 165 been scored?

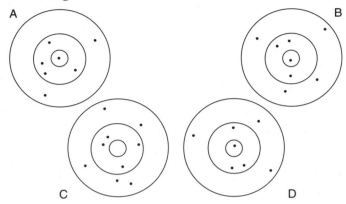

7   A sculptor started with a slab of marble weighing 450 kg. The first week he chiselled 40% away, the second week he chiselled half what he had left away and on the final week he completed his statue by chiselling another ninth of what he had left away.

What was the weight of the final statue?

8   What number should replace the question mark?

6	8	6	2	4
2	9	7	8	9
9	8	?	1	3

9   Sue had half as many again as Fred, and Pat had a third as many again as Sue. Altogether they had 216. How many did each have?

10 My meal and the drinks cost £50. If the meal had cost £10 more, the drinks would have been a third of the total. If the drinks had been £10 less, I would have spent 75% of the total on the meal.

How much did the meal cost?

Answers to IQ test one

Spatial ability test

1 D; there are two separate sequences: the first arrow
   rotates through 180° at each stage and the second arrow
   rotates 90° anti-clockwise.

2 B; assuming the line which splits the box in two is a
   mirror, both sides are a correct mirror-image.

3 D

4 A; the rest are all the same figure rotated.

5 F; looking both across and down the content of the final
   square is determined by the contents of the first two
   squares. All lines from the first two squares are carried
   forward to the final square except when two lines appear
   in the same position, in which case they are cancelled
   out.

6 B: looking across, lines are in identical positions and the
   dot occupies four different positions.

7 B; another rectangle is added at each stage at 90° to the
   previous one, working clockwise.

8 C; the large circle moves one place clockwise at each
   stage, and the small circle moves two places anti-
   clockwise.

9 B; lines are carried forward to the final circle only when
   they appear in the same position in the first two circles,
   but then straight lines become curved and vice versa.

10 D; the three figures are being repeated and every fourth figure is inverted.

Logic test

1 edition; each word begins with the same three letters that end the word before, albeit in a different order.

2 Jack

3 7416; all the others are in anagram pairs, that is they use the same four digits, 4728/7482, 3954/4359, 8612/1268, 3621/1326.

4 211213; each number 'describes' the number before, starting with its smallest digits, i.e. 121 contains two 1s and one 2, so the next number is 2112; 1132 contains two 1s, one 2 and one 3.

5 ideas; to complete a magic word square: REMIT
                                             ELUDE
                                             MUSER
                                             IDEAS
                                             TERSE

6 48193; reverse the first number and reduce the middle digit by 1.

7 8; add the first two triangles together to produce the numbers in the third triangle, i.e. 3 + 2 = 5, 4 + 3 = 7; thus 2 + 6 = 8.

8 LED: N m L   T s   R
          E fgh I   A bcd E
          W vu T   G fe D

9 ABDGK: ABcDefGhijK

10 invoke; the end of one word and the beginning of
   another form another word:
   ex(tra de)are(st ray)o(n est)abli(sh in)voke.

Verbal ability test
  1 atrocious

  2 potent, weak

  3 repressive, democratic

  4 paroxysm

  5 d) left-handed

  6 Today, some of the worst cases of verbosity are found in
    academia where arguments are judged to be more
    impressive the longer it takes to express them.

  7 debut; it is a start word, where all the rest are concluding
    words.

  8 be in awe of

  9 querulous, petulant

10 d) tit for tat

Numerical ability test
  1 23 minutes

  2 5; 12 + 23 = 35, 35/5 = 7

  3 122; add all the previous digits to the last number,
    including the digits of the last number itself.

4 71; 75 − 71 = 4, square root of 4 = 2

5 2 and 1:

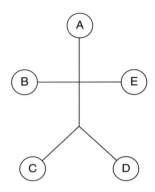

A × B = number formed by digits of C and D, A × C = E

6 B

7 120 kg

8 4; 68624 + 29789 = 98413

9 Fred 48, Sue 72, Pat 96

10 £30

Meal	Drinks	Total
£30	£20	£50
£40	£20	£60
£30	£10	£40

IQ test two

1 What is ECARTE?

    a) type of curtains
    b) an omelette
    c) a card game
    d) a church service
    e) a sundae

2 What do these have in common?

    a) a soothsayer
    b) griffon
    c) kaolin
    d) mugged
    e) tundra

3 Place two three-letter bits together to make an animal.

    CON   BUF   MAN   ALO   MAR   RAC   CAY   MOS

4 Make this into a word:

    – – – K K E E – – –

5 Fill in the missing letters to make two words which are synonyms.

6 Fill in the blanks to find five islands.

a) . R . N . D .
b) . U . A . R .
c) . O . M . S .
d) . N . I . U .
e) . A . R . I .

7 All of the vowels have been omitted from this trite saying. Can you replace them?

FTFRS TYDNT SCCDG VP

8 Make a six-letter word using only these four letters:.

F O
C E

9 Find a ten-letter word by moving from circle to circle, only entering each circle once.

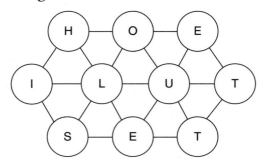

10 Place the letters in the grid to find two animals.

B C F I L
L O K U Y

Numerical ability test

1 **What number should replace the question mark?**

18, 1, 14¾, 5¾, 11½, 10½, ?

2 Simplify

$$\frac{7}{8} \div \frac{28}{32}$$

3 Simplify

14 − 1½ × 3½ + 3 × ½

4 **What number should replace the question mark?**

48	8	2	12
39	13	3	9
12	2	2	12
15	5	7	?

5 What does this mathematical sign mean?

!

6 What number should replace the question mark?

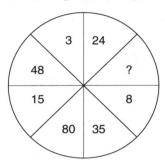

7 Change 86°F to Celsius.

8 What is the value of the angle of the octagon?

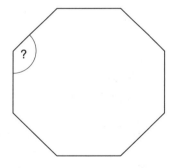

9 Change 0.126$\overline{333}$ to a fraction.

10 If   66 = 102
   then 22 =   ?

Maths

1 Three tramps met in the country. One had three loaves of bread, one had two loaves of bread, and the third had no loaves at all, but had £1. The loaves were shared equally. How much did the third tramp pay the other two?

2 Two square floors had to be tiled, covered in 12 ins. square tiles. The total number of tiles used was 850.

   Each side of one floor was 10 feet more than the other floor.

   What were the dimensions of the two floors?

3 Two cards are dealt from a shuffled pack. What are the odds that one of the cards dealt will be of a named suit?

4 Boxes 1 + 2 weigh 12 kg
   Boxes 2 + 3 weigh 13.5 kg
   Boxes 3 + 4 weigh 11.5 kg
   Boxes 4 + 5 weigh 8 kg
   Boxes 1 + 3 + 5 weigh 16 kg

   How much did each box weigh?

5 A wine shop has wine at £9.50 a bottle, and cheaper wine at £5.50 a bottle.

   How many bottles of wine must be mixed together to sell wine at £7.90 a bottle and still make the same profit?

6 If   81 = 90
   then 22 = ?

7 All recurring decimals are generated by fractions. Which fraction generates this decimal?

0. 818444

8 Simplify

$$\frac{15}{19} \div \frac{30}{57}$$

9 What number should replace the question mark?

6	26	8	4
9	21	10	3
7	20	9	3
15	40	11	?

10 Simplify

$17 - 8 \times 2 + 15 \div 2$

Diagrams

1   Symbols

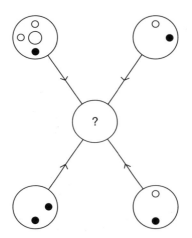

Each line and symbol which appears in the four outer circles, above, is transferred to the centre circle according to these rules:

If a line or symbol occurs in the outer circles:

once:	it is transferred
twice:	it is possibly transferred
three times:	it is transferred
four times:	it is not transferred

Which of the circles shown below should appear at the centre of the diagram, above?

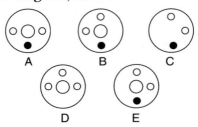

2   Symbols

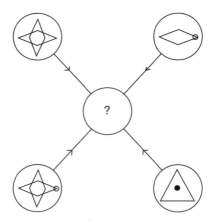

Each line and symbol which appears in the four outer
circles, above, is transferred to the centre circle
according to these rules:

If a line or symbol occurs in the outer circles:

once: it is transferred
twice: it is possibly transferred
three times: it is transferred
four times: it is not transferred

Which of the circles shown below should appear
at the centre of the diagram, above?

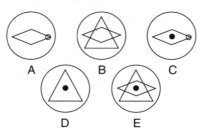

3   Grid

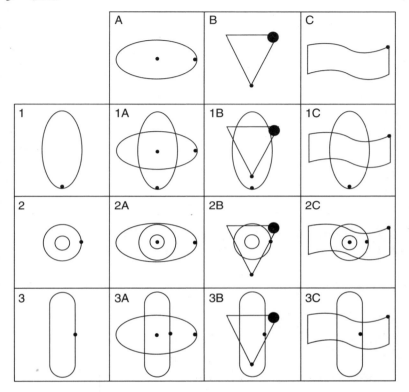

Each of the nine squares in the grid marked 1A to 3C should incorporate all the lines and symbols which are shown in the squares of the same letter and number immediately above and to the left. For example, 2B should incorporate all the lines and symbols that are in 2 and B.

One of the squares is incorrect. Which one is it?

4   Grid

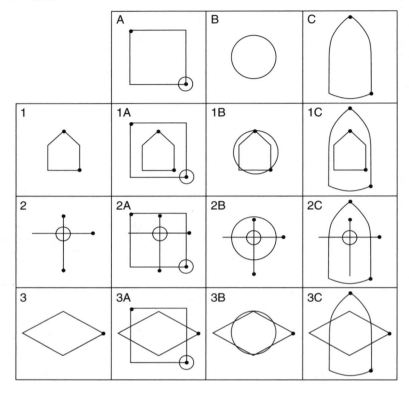

Each of the nine squares in the grid marked 1A to 3C should incorporate all the lines and symbols which are shown in the squares of the same letter and number immediately above and to the left. For example, 2B should incorporate all the lines and symbols that are in 2 and B.

One of the squares is incorrect. Which one is it?

5   Which is the odd one out?

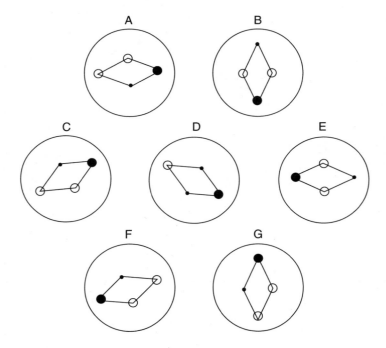

6 Which is the odd one out?

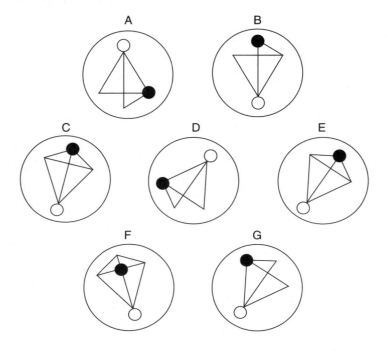

7   Circles

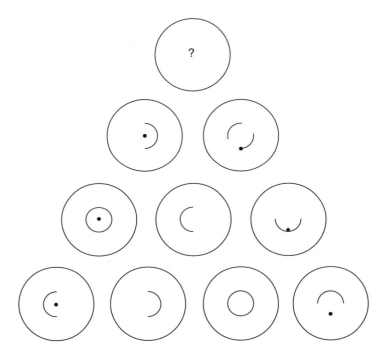

Which circle should replace the question mark?

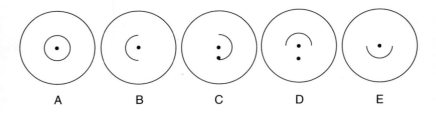

A   B   C   D   E

8   Circles

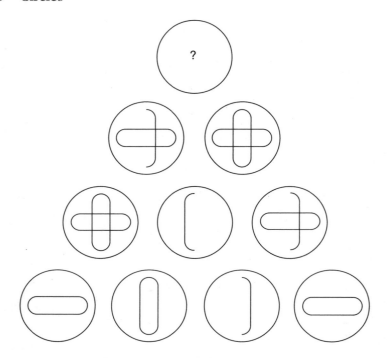

Which circle should replace the question mark?

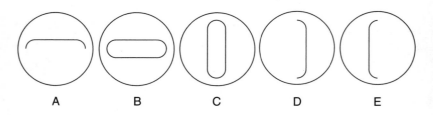

A   B   C   D   E

9   Hexagons

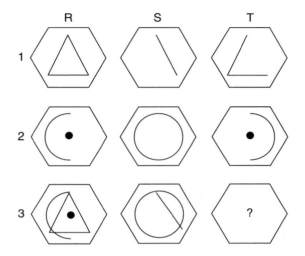

Which hexagon should replace the question mark?

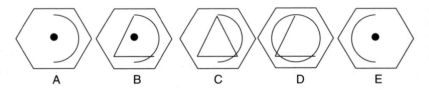

10 Hexagons

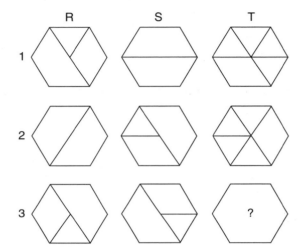

Which hexagon should replace the question mark?

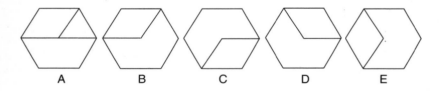

Answers to IQ test two

Verbal ability test
1 c) A card game

2 They all contain the names of trees spelled backwards:
    ASH, FIR, OAK, GUM, NUT

3 cayman

4 bookkeeper

5 bunglers, failures

6 a) Grenada
    b) Sumatra
    c) Formosa
    d) Antigua
    e) Bahrain

7 If at first you don't succeed give up

8 coffee

9 silhouette

10 bullock, filly

Numerical ability test
1 There are two series:

   $- 3\frac{1}{4}$ 18, $14\frac{3}{4}$, $11\frac{1}{2}$, $8\frac{1}{4}$
   $+ 4\frac{3}{4}$ 1, $5\frac{3}{4}$, $10\frac{1}{2}$

   Answer = $8\frac{1}{4}$

2    $\dfrac{7}{8} \times \dfrac{32}{28} = 1$

3    $14 - 5\frac{1}{4} + 1\frac{1}{2} = 10\frac{1}{4}$

   $(\times, \div)$ must be evaluated before $(+, -)$

4   21; $(15 \div 5) \times 7 = 21$

5   Factorial: $6! = 6 \times 5 \times 4 \times 3 \times 2 \times 1$

6   63; squares – 1, jump 2 segments:

   $2^2 - 1 = 3, 3^2 - 1 = 8, 4^2 - 1 = 15, 5^2 - 1 = 24,$
   $6^2 - 1 = 35, 7^2 - 1 = 48, 8^2 - 1 = 63, 9^2 - 1 = 80$

7   30 °C; $86 - 32 = 54 \times \frac{5}{9} = 30$ °C

8   135°; $\dfrac{360°}{8} = 45°;$ $180° - 45° = 135°$

9    $\begin{array}{rl} \times 1 & = \quad 0.126333 \\ \times 1000 & = \underline{126.333333} \\ 999 & = \overline{126.207} \end{array}$

   Answer $= \dfrac{126.207}{999}$

10   66 = 102 (MOD8): $\begin{array}{rl} 1 \times 64 = & 64 \\ 0 \times \ 8 = & \ 0 \\ 2 \times \ 1 = & \underline{\ 2} \\ & 66 \end{array}$

   22 = 26 (MOD8): $\begin{array}{rl} 2 \times \ 8 = & 16 \\ 6 \times \ 1 = & \underline{\ 6} \\ & 22 \end{array}$

Maths

1   Each tramp had ⅗ loaves. The third tramp gave 80p to the first and 20p to the second.

2   25 ft × 25 ft
    15 ft × 15 ft

3   First draw: $\dfrac{13}{52} = 0.25$

   Second draw: $\dfrac{39}{52} \times \dfrac{13}{51} = \dfrac{507}{2652} = 0.1912$

   (Assuming that first draw was not successful)

   The odds are therefore $(0.25 + 0.1912) = 0.4412$, or 44.12%

4   Box 1   5.5 kg
    Box 2   6.5 kg
    Box 3   7.0 kg
    Box 4   4.5 kg
    Box 5   3.5 kg

5   3 at £9.50 and 2 at £5.50

6   81 (MOD10) = 90 (MOD9): $9 \times 9 = 81$
                               $0 \times 1 = \underline{0}$
                               81

   22 (MOD10) = 24 (MOD9): $2 \times 9 = 18$
                              $4 \times 1 = \underline{4}$
                              22

7   0. 818444   1 =   0.818444
                  1000 = 818.444444
                   999 = 817.626

   Answer = $\dfrac{817.626}{999}$

8 $\dfrac{15}{19} \times \dfrac{57}{30} = \dfrac{3}{2} = 1\frac{1}{2}$

9 5; $\dfrac{15 + 40}{11} = 5$

10 $17 - 16 + 7\frac{1}{2} = 8\frac{1}{2}$

(×, ÷) must be evaluated before (+, –)

Diagrams

1 B

2 E

3 2A

4 2C

5 D; A is the same as F
     B is the same as E
     C is the same as G

6 F; A is the same as G
     B is the same as D
     C is the same as E

7 D; each circle is obtained by joining the two circles below, but similar portions disappear.

8 E; each circle is obtained by joining the two circles below, but similar portions disappear.

9 B; R is added to S to equal T, but similar portions disappear; 1 is added to 2 to equal 3.

10 C; R is added to S to equal T, but similar portions disappear; 1 is added to 2 to equal 3, but similar portions disappear.

The IQ Workout Series

PHILIP CARTER and KEN RUSSELL, UK Mensa Puzzle Editors

Available from all good bookshops or direct from

John Wiley & Sons Ltd, Distribution Centre, 1 Oldlands Way, Bognor Regis, West Sussex, PO22 9SA

DIAL FREE (UK only) 0800 243407 or (for overseas orders) +44 1243 843294,
cs-books@wiley.co.uk

www.wiley.co.uk

2382a